SMALL
TREES
FOR GARDENS

Mountain ash trees are primarily grown for their generous clusters of late summer fruits and their autumn leaf colour. *Sorbus aucuparia* 'Xanthocarpa', here, is a yellow-fruited variety.

SMALL TREES FOR GARDENS

Ann Bonar

WARD LOCK LIMITED · LONDON

ACKNOWLEDGEMENTS

The publishers gratefully acknowledge the following agencies and photographers for granting permission to reproduce the colour photographs: Pat Brindley (pp. 2, 10, 14, 26, 27 (both), 31 (upper), & 66; John Glover (p. 11); Photos Horticultural Picture Library (pp. 15, 34, 38, 46 & 54); Peter McHoy (front cover and pp. 19, 23, 31 (lower), & 42; and Andrew Lawson (p. 43).

All the line drawings are by Nils Solberg.

© Ward Lock Limited 1989
First published in Great Britain in 1989
by Ward Lock Limited, 8 Clifford Street,
London W1X 1RB.

House editor Denis Ingram

Text filmset in Bembo
by Hourds Typographica, Stafford

Printed and bound in Portugal
by Resopal

British Library Cataloguing in Publication Data

Bonar, Ann
    Small trees for gardens.
    1. Gardens. Trees
    I. Title
    635.9'77
    ISBN 0-7063-6745-6

CONTENTS

PREFACE

Trees are at a premium in the world nowadays; too many are being cut down daily for any of us to be complacent about the reasons for felling them, such as commercial use or even the need for land. Whatever we can do to replace them in our gardens can only help the environment.

Trees can be defined as woody plants with a single main stem from ground level, whereas shrubs have several stems coming from the same point at ground level. However, some trees have short main stems or trunks, with branches originating low down, perhaps only 60 or 90 cm (2 or 3 ft) above the soil, and then they look like shrubby trees. Others can easily have a standard trunk, but the branches sweep out sideways and then down, covering a substantial circumference round the trunk and making it difficult to grow anything else beneath them.

In this book I have described over 100 small trees whose height will be about 9 m (30 ft) at maturity. Each has at least one visual merit, and in many cases there are two, or even more; some have the bonus of appeal to our stomachs as well as our eyes, in the form of edible fruits.

The descriptions of these trees are in an alphabetical list, which is accompanied by chapters on the use of small trees in garden design in each season of the year, a review of their uses, and chapters on the practical aspects of growing them. There are also lists of trees for a variety of purposes and situations. Whether the reader has a small or large garden, he or she should be able to find a suitable small tree or trees.

The eventual height of a particular species can vary a good deal. The heights given here are average, but so much depends on the soil, the position, the climate, and the closeness of other trees and plants, that deviation from the figure can be considerable. Rate of growth each year is supplied in the individual descriptions, and this is a good guide, remembering that it will be faster for the first ten years or so than in later life. Some control of the final height can be obtained with pruning to take out the leading shoot some way below that required.

Some species for tropical and sub-tropical climates have been included as it is possible to grow these in sheltered temperate gardens. The smaller palms, for instance, are delightful. Those described should be easy to obtain, ornamental value for space, and not difficult to grow.

A.B.

CHAPTER 1

PRACTICAL USES IN THE GARDEN

In islands as far apart as Crete in the Mediterranean and Easter Island in the Pacific, there are tree deserts. Once, both islands were heavily forested, but the Cretan trees were cut down to build ships, and the Polynesian jungles – mostly palms – were destroyed in a slash-and-burn agriculture. Now the terrain is bare, and the exposed soil is gradually being eroded, down to rock. The populations of both islands have decreased severely as a result, and whole cultures have disappeared.

Trees are no less essential to gardens, whatever the size of garden, not necessarily for construction or survival, but for other reasons just as important to the garden owner, and indirectly to the neighbouring environment. Some of their uses are modified by their size – for instance the choice of a large tree in a garden may simply be because of the sheer volume of its presence. Small trees arguably have more qualities to suit them for the general run of gardens, whereas forest trees will overpower anything but a grand landscape. They can actually be rather intimidating, too.

Trees are rather arbitrarily divided into three groups: small, medium-sized and large trees. Here we are concerned only with the first-named, and their size can be from 2 m (6½ ft) or so, up to 9 m (30 ft). There seems to be a no-man's-land between 9 and 12 m (30 and 40 ft), which includes both large 'small trees', and small 'medium-sized' trees. In practice small trees which can grow taller than 9 m (30 ft) in good soils and benevolent climates are often sneaked into the 'small' category, not quite justifiably, by nurserymen. It pays therefore to keep a close eye on catalogue descriptions where the height is often given as so many metres (or feet) after *ten* years. If the rate of growth is 60 cm (2 ft) a year, beware!

Small trees are a great deal less damaging to the domestic surroundings of a garden. Their canopy of top growth casts less shade, and the shade there is, is usually less dense. The roots do not demand so much food and water, and their size does not overwhelm the design of a garden, nor does it overpower the kind of plants grown in one. The medium to large trees make much more sense in a landscape garden of many acres, but the interesting point here is that small trees can still be fitted into such designs in some of the ways suggested in the next chapter.

SHELTER

One of the prime functions of trees in gardens is to provide shelter. In many cases this is shelter from wind, to be able to put leafy hands firmly in the face of cold northerlies or easterlies without incurring frostbite. They also provide a barricade against the steady prevailing winds which can destroy soft garden plants, and even mould all but the strongest trees into the frozen silhouettes which give away its direction. Their canopies ensure warmth by deflecting the wind; the sun's heat and light are filtered, and snow and frost on the plants beneath them and nearby are ameliorated.

Evergreen trees are particularly good at providing shelter from all these natural hazards, and have the further advantage that an annual leaf-fall does not have to be dealt with in some way. Even so, it should be remembered that the adjective does not mean that a leaf, once produced, remains on the tree until the tree dies. Evergreens shed their leaves just as deciduous species do, but not all at once in autumn. They are not killed by frost, but survive into the following growing season, and may then come to a natural end, falling in ones and twos, perhaps in a shower of the oldest in spring as new ones develop, but never so many at any time that the tree is bare, whether in patches or completely.

TREES FOR SCREENING

Trees can provide shelter in the form of screens as well as single specimens, and some of the conifers are particularly good for this purpose, such as *Chamaecyparis lawsoniana* (Lawson cypress), with variously coloured foliage depending on the cultivar. Such screens have a two-fold purpose, since they can act as boundaries against the outside world and define the limit of the garden, doing duty as a living wall costing a good deal less than the inert kind. Limits can also be marked, less intensively, by deciduous trees with bare trunks, such as *Sorbus aucuparia* (mountain ash), laburnum or *Cercis siliquastrum* (Judas tree). The tamarix sprouts water shoots from its main trunk with enormous alacrity, making a much more continuous screen beneath the main trunks and, if the garden is mild and the climate right, pittosporum or *Arbutus unedo* (the strawberry tree) will close even more gaps.

But trees are primarily for defining areas and suggesting boundaries. They are not hedges and not intended as full-scale 'green' fences. They can indicate divisions within gardens without actually cutting off a view or enclosing a space, a useful characteristic when a hedge is too time-consuming or a wall or fence is inappropriate.

TREES FOR PRIVACY

A population which lives largely in towns and cities cannot avoid close associations with other buildings than its own, and even the country gardener, living in a village, can be unwillingly overlooked or overshadowed by a neighbour. But this is where small trees show one of their greatest assets: species which screen or block out the nearby houses, garages, stables and all the other clutter.

There is a good choice in tree heights, up to 9 m (30 ft). The head of the tree can be spreading, bushy, weeping, vase-shaped or upright (fastigiate) and, since some trees clothe themselves down to ground level, the habit of growth may be conical, pyramidal or columnar. Year-round privacy will be ensured if an evergreen is planted. A judicial combination of these features will screen expanses of blank wall and potentially prying windows without overstepping the limits of good neighbourliness.

The rate at which this screening occurs varies enormously from species to species, and is important to consider if screening is one of the purposes of planting. Trees have many years in which to mature, unlike herbaceous perennials or annuals. If they come from the warmer parts of the world they are likely to grow more quickly, even in cool temperate climates, than those from near the Polar borders, such as some of the willows. However, as with so many gardening generalizations, this is not a hard-and-fast rule. Some of the northern conifers put on 60 cm (2 ft) a year, and × *Cupressocyparis leylandii* (Leyland cypress), with *Chamaecyparis nootkatensis* (Nootka cypress) from Alaska in its parentage, elongates annually by about a yard. But the majority increase by about 30–45 cm (1–1½ ft), and some are much slower.

TREES AND THE ENVIRONMENT

The contribution of trees to their environment is immense. For instance where would birds be without trees? True, there are shrubs, but nests in these are frequently too close to the ground to be comfortable and safe from four-legged hunters. Besides protection, trees provide food, material for nests, perches, warmth in winter and shelter from the wind.

Trees provide habitats for an altogether different collection of insect fauna, in the shape of moths, beetles, caterpillars, flies, aphids and so on. Squirrels will visit them and may even make dreys in them. Their leaves provide a vast natural source of humus, marvellous material for compost heaps. The light in the garden is broken up by trees casting dappled or unbroken shade, and so creating new conditions for different types of plants. The way in which they fill vertical space is another aspect.

CHAPTER 2

TREES IN GARDEN DESIGN

One's mental picture of a tree is of a plant with a single, vertical, hard-wood stem topped by a collection of leafy branches, the whole taller than it is wide, and in general with the branches at least higher than head height. But when you look into this more closely, you will find that there are so often variations on it that the conventional tree shape hardly seems to exist. As soon as this is realized, there is at once tremendous scope for placing trees in the existing garden design. In a flash it becomes

The weeping birch, *Betula pendula* 'Youngii', is a graceful small tree with the typical white-barked trunk of this popular species.

Cotoneaster 'Hybridus Pendulus' bears heavy crops of rich scarlet berries on a 1.8–2.1 m (6–7 ft) tall weeping tree.

much more fun and much more exhilarating to discover the possibilities in forms and growth habits.

Regardless of the shape of the tree, however, it is primarily a vertical plant, larger than the others in the garden, and it makes use of vertical space, three-dimensionally, unlike wall plants which tend to be in two planes only. Whatever your reasons for wanting a tree, one of them will be to give height to the design, and being permanent plants, trees suit this task admirably. Herbaceous plants die down, shrubs are not tall enough and literally cover too much soil, climbers cannot function without support. But with tree plantings, a flat design is translated from a horizontal, almost unreal, picture, to a reality with substance and volume.

TREE SHAPES

But besides giving height to your garden landscape, a tree can contribute further interest by its shape or silhouette – much more so than a shrub, which has much less architectural value in its bun-like outline.

FASTIGIATE
It would seem unlikely that a tree could be more vertical than it already is, but some are just this, and are described as fastigiate. This is derived from the Latin, *fastigium*, or *fastigiatus*, literally sloping down, as with a roof or the gable end of a roof. If you turn it on its head, it can also mean 'narrowed to a point', which exactly describes a Lombardy poplar or an Italian cypress. These extremely narrow forms lend themselves to small spaces where height is wanted but width is almost unavailable. There is the variety of juniper called *Juniperus* 'Skyrocket', and that of the Japanese flowering cherry *Prunus* 'Erecta' (syn. 'Ama-no-gawa'), both narrow small trees eligible to be called fastigiate. Both would look decorative, the cherry with its pink flowers, the juniper with its blue-green foliage, planted in a grey-paved patio or courtyard where the formal horizontal lines of the paving would complement the vertical habit of the trees. They are also good trees for narrow borders at the side of drives, and make especially good focal points in lawns.

ROUNDED
Many trees have heads – the collection of branches at the top of the trunk – which are rounded or spread horizontally, drooping with age almost to ground level. Those which keep their branches well up above the ground provide our conventional view of a tree and can be inserted into the garden plan in all sorts of ways. Specimen trees, carefully chosen for

shape, flowering, autumn colour and so on, are best shown off in a lawn planting where the eye is not distracted from the clean lines of the trunk by woolly mixtures of bulbs, groundcover and perennials planted beneath them. A sweep of smoothly shaven grass in front and behind, however small, will provide an unrivalled backdrop to a flowering malus (crab apple) or a graceful eucryphia. A blue conifer, for example *Picea pungens* 'Koster' or *Chamaecyparis lawsoniana* 'Columnaris', will give immense visual pleasure in a lawn, when the branches and foliage spread down to ground level.

FOCAL POINT

Lawn planting is not the only way of drawing attention to a tree. The eye can also be drawn to them by making them the focal point in a particular part of the garden, such as the end of a pathway, a silhouette against the horizon, an attention-catcher beside a pool, or a site where autumn leaf colour will be caught by the setting sun. Small, fastigiate trees make particularly good focal points and give more emphasis to formal surroundings.

VASE-SHAPED

Some trees are vase-shaped, a very useful quality if the planting area is restricted. You can be sure that the branches will be well above ground level, and yet the trees still have a tree-like form. Later they will open out to give more shade as the tree matures but will still not get in the way lower down. More conventionally shaped trees can easily carry branches drooping down to the soil and taking up a large area which might otherwise serve for planting or sitting. The 'Ukon' variety of Japanese cherry is one example of this habit of growth, with sulphur-yellow flowers and bronzy green leaves in spring. Others are the laburnum, which when well matured eventually has branches drooping at the ends, and the crab apple 'John Downie', also arching with age, but well above the ground.

COLUMNS AND PYRAMIDS

You can also make good use of the columnar and pyramidal shapes, which cover themselves with branches and foliage down to ground level. Often they are conifers, for instance *Chamaecyparis lawsoniana* 'Columnaris' (Lawson cypress), whose green foliage is blue-grey tinged, or the picea called 'Hoopsii', also column-shaped. The pyramidal *Laurus nobilis* (sweet bay) is evergreen and sweeps down to the soil, a good specimen for a sheltered sunny spot. *Prunus incisa* (Fuji cherry) can develop a pyramidal head as it matures, well above the soil, and so can most of the hollies. *Sorbus aucuparia* 'Asplenifolia' (fern-leaved mountain ash), is

Prunus 'Erecta' ('Ama-no-gawa'), decked in pale pink blossom in spring, is valued particularly for its narrow columnar shape.

another, and the beautiful *Magnolia kobus* carries its upright white flowers on branches that form a cone when young, then become spreading with age, but always well above the ground.

RELATING TREES TO GARDEN FEATURES

Whatever shape and type of tree you choose for the garden, besides taking into account its needs as regards soil, light, aspect and spacing, consider how it will relate to the other garden features nearby. Too close to a herbaceous border, and it will cover the plants in leaves in autumn and starve them of light and moisture while growing. It can also distract the eye from the border, as well as blunting its own impact. But, situated behind the border, perhaps halfway along it, with a seat in its shade,

A weeping silver-leaved pear, *Pyrus salicifolia* 'Pendula', here contrasts well with a variegated Norway maple, *Acer platanoides* 'Drummondii' in the background.

neither overwhelms the other, and each can be appreciated separately for its own merits.

Terraces and patios can only have their atmosphere of leisure and tranquillity enhanced by a tree planted nearby, shading them from the heat of the sun and providing a buffer against disturbing breezes. Such trees should not be too large, otherwise they could cut out the light from the house windows or overwhelm the terrace, and something with an architectural air to it would blend appropriately – a magnolia or a tabulate cornus or, for a complete change of style, *Cercis siliquastrum* (Judas tree) or one of the malus (crab apple) species.

Pergolas are such splendid features in their own right that competition with them needs to be avoided. Trees planted close to them are impractical for a variety of reasons anyway, not least that the trees lose their individuality. Trees and pergolas associated with one another make for fuss and overwhelm the eye – there is too much to take in and the result is that nothing is appreciated. After some years, the roots of vigorous trees might disturb the foundations of the pergola too.

Steps are a different matter altogether. A flight of steps lends itself admirably to a tree planting at the top – the eye will automatically be carried up the steps, and actually needs a focus to finish with, if there is not to be a sense of anti-climax. Such a position is marvellous for one of the focal points referred to earlier. It could be a 'sit-under' tree such as *Robinia pseudoacacia* 'Frisia' (golden false acacia), or it can be a 'sit-beside' – *Prunus* 'Cheal's Weeping' (weeping cherry) or a camellia.

Some other garden features with which trees are difficult to associate are walls, gazebos and arbours, perhaps because they use up space vertically as well. Boundary and dividing walls supply homes most readily for true climbing plants or for plants, especially shrubs, needing protection, but the single trunk of a tree does little to break up the blank expanse of a wall. If you use a shrubby type of tree, it tends to become a shrub to the casual glance – two verticals don't make a tree. To give a tree any distinction at all by a wall, it needs to be planted by a wrought-iron gate which provides a space to see through into another part of the garden. Then tree, gate and view can all be balanced without detracting from one another.

Gazebos and arbours are artefacts with definite characters of their own. Plant a tree close by, and it will either not be noticed, or will belittle both, so that they recede from the scene. The nearest you might get to a tree in the area would be a weeping form, but even this needs to be carefully chosen and sited – some varieties reach 3.6 m (12 ft) tall and as much wide, making an excellent natural substitute for either feature! So be sure of the eventual dimensions before choosing.

WEEPING TREES

Weeping trees usually take the form in which the branches trail down to ground level, forming an umbrella- or dome-shaped head. Other species produce branches which arch over and become pendulous quite high up on the tree – they are still described as weeping but not in the sense that is usually accepted. Laburnums and *Betula pendula* 'Youngii' (Young's silver birch) are both examples of this type of weeping habit, and they make graceful and particularly attractive trees.

Weeping species which go the whole hog do not necessarily turn into completely enclosed leafy grottoes. *Salix purpurea* 'Pendula' and *S. caprea* 'Kilmarnock' (small weeping willow) will do so, and so will *Fraxinus excelsior* 'Pendula' (weeping ash) and *Pyrus salicifolia* 'Pendula' (willow-leaved pear), but 'Cheal's Weeping Cherry' trails long garlands of flowers separately down to the soil so that it is possible to see the garden through a framework of blossom. *Cotoneaster* 'Hybridus Pendulus' (weeping cotoneaster) follows suit, but wreathed in bright red berries. Neither tree ever completely closes itself in.

The gigantic, commonly planted *Salix* 'Chrysocoma' (weeping willow), called golden because of its yellow-barked young shoots, is often planted beside water, partly because a moist soil suits it best, and partly because its form is enhanced by reflection. This weeping habit is pretty beside water, whatever the species of tree, especially the cherry already referred to, and *Betula pendula* 'Youngii' (silver birch).

For planting on the bank of a stream, or in moist soil anywhere, a willow is ideal and, although the common weeping form is too big, there are two others that remain as small trees – a weeping form of *Salix caprea* (goat or pussy willow) called 'Kilmarnock', and *S. purpurea* 'Pendula' (purple-barked willow). If you want a small specimen tree for a lawn, 'weepers' are always suitable, varying in height from about 1.8–3.6 m (6–12 ft) and with the same spread, usually rather slow-growing.

GROUP PLANTING

Small trees are planted mainly for their ornamental value, and so are generally grown as single specimens. But if the space is available there is no reason why they should not be used to form a copse or wood. A grove of *Arbutus unedo* (strawberry trees), a miniature woodland of camellias or a mixed collection of malus and prunus (crab apples and ornamental cherries) are all possibilities. Acers (maples) with their coloured autumn leaves, and *Sorbus aucuparia* (mountain ashes) would set off the evergreen ilex (hollies) in a group, and all would be happy with the same soil and site.

CHAPTER 3

SPRING PARADE

Spring is a time when Nature overdoes it, as so often in the plant world. What a waste it always seems not to sow all those seeds that a poppy produces, and what a pity not to let all those borage or even sycamore seedlings continue to live and grow, once they have germinated. On second thoughts, perhaps we can be hard-hearted about the sycamore seedlings, for they are but weeds and a plain green-leaved sycamore can grow to 30 m (100 ft).

EARLY SPRING DISPLAY

Willows

Spring is the beginning of that particular stage in a plant's life-cycle, and amongst the first of the trees to move into new growth are salix (willows), a rather neglected group of trees known mostly for the forest-sized weeping willow and the 'palm' which appears around Easter. But it would be worth finding out more about them. There are tiny creeping shrublets, species with round, woolly, and contorted, twisted leaves, as well as the familiar silvery-green narrow kind, varieties with red, yellow and purple twigs, and not a few which keep to a modest tree height. Willows for osiers, *Salix caerulea* (cricket-bat willow) and *S. pentandra* (willow with scented leaves) and *S. lanata*, the shrubby woolly willow with a soft woolly covering to the young growth and vertical male catkins, golden and 5 cm (2 in) long, are a few more.

But two which are charming in early spring and easily obtained – you will have to take time to track down the more unusual willows – are *S. caprea* 'Pendula' and *S. purpurea* 'Kilmarnock'. Both are small 'weepers'. The former is a weeping goat or pussy willow whose silky grey gold-tipped male catkins appear first, up to 2.5 cm (1 in) long and rather rounded compared with the females, which open on separate plants and are twice as long but less attractive. The purple osier also produces catkins on the bare branches, but its chief interest is the shining purple bark of the young growth, effective and eye-catching for most of the season, especially on this weeping form, and when it is combined with the blue-green leaves.

A *Laburnum* 'Vossii' looks a picture when in full bloom in May, but the more so when it reinforces a lovely display of wallflowers, as here.

Camellias

In sheltered gardens, you may find the exquisitely flowered camellias bursting the fat buds which formed the previous autumn at the same time as the pussy willow appears. *Camellia japonica* is hardy enough to survive hard frost, even without a blanket of snow, and its hybrids will flower at their best protected from wind and the early morning sun. Dappled shade seems to suit them very well, and it would be difficult to find a more glamorous flowering tree – some would say a shrub, but they do ultimately grow tall. In warm temperate climates, *C. reticulata* will grow out of doors, and is an even more beautiful plant, with such tempting names as 'Butterfly Wings', 'Shot Silk' and 'Chang's Temple'. The number of hybrids runs into hundreds, and their attraction is such that camellia societies have been formed all over the world. With neutral or acid soil you should really fill the garden with them, in preference to rhododendrons, which are nowhere near as ornamental out of flower as the glossy, laurel-leaved camellias.

Robinia

For a complete contrast to these two, the false acacia follows them as its leaves unfold late in early spring. *Robinia pseudoacacia* 'Frisia', also called the locust tree, was an outstanding find in a Dutch nursery in the thirties. The species is green-leaved and grows into a largish tree with hanging clusters of white, fragrant, sweetpea-shaped flowers, but its cultivar does not grow anywhere near as tall, and the delicate feathery leaves are golden-yellow throughout the growing season. Combined with the flowers, it makes a glorious specimen, especially with a background of dark green evergreen, such as yew or holly. Its only drawback – a minor one – is that the wood is brittle, so a position away from the wind is preferable.

MID SPRING

Acer

Another tree, very much smaller, grown for its foliage, is *Acer pseudoplatanus* 'Brilliantissimum'. Like the willows, this genus forms a large group of hardy deciduous trees, with many forest giants – *A. pseudoplatanus* (sycamore), *A. rubrum* (Canadian maple), *A. saccharum* (sugar maple) and *A. platanoides* (Norway maple) amongst them – but also includes tiny trees, more like shrubs, such as the Japanese maples, also grown for their foliage. *Acer* 'Brilliantissimum' is enchanting, as its shrimp-pink buds elongate until they are much the same shape as shrimps, and then burst into pleated leaves, lobed and pointed, of a deeper rosy salmon shade, slowly turning green as the summer progresses. The head becomes mushroom shaped and, with advanced age, dome-shaped, on a tree very slowly growing to 9 m (30 ft), occasionally more. An added attraction are the dangling clusters of pale yellow 'keys'. The *A. negundo* 'Variegatum' (variegated box elder), is another good maple which does not get out of hand. It has a graceful branching habit sweeping down practically to ground level, and its white-edged leaves enhance the airy impression.

Amelanchier

In small spaces every plant should pay its way decoratively for as much of the year as possible. Sometimes a single season of beauty is so outstanding that a tree can be forgiven for a quiet appearance the rest of the year, as with prunus (Japanese cherries), but *Amelanchier lamarckii* (snowy mespilus or June berry) has a constant succession of attractions. *A. lamarckii* (syn. *A. canadensis, A. laevis*) has a twiggy head. It is not a substantial tree carrying thick, heavy branches, but more a tracery of shoots and slender boughs well suited to the white blossom clustered all along them in mid spring. Before this, however, the leaves and new shoots unfold a reddish bronze, so that the leaves and flowers together make an elegant and unusual show. The small round fruits which follow the flowers change colour from their initial green, deepening through shades of red to black, when they are juicy, sweet and edible. In autumn the leaves change to deep yellows and reds before they fall. Altogether the snowy mespilus puts on a constantly changing display of colour from early spring until well into autumn.

Judas tree

The snowy mespilus is a North American native. The tree which flowers along with it or just as it finishes, by contrast, comes from South-Eastern Europe. *Cercis siliquastrum* (the Judas tree) is always attractive, whether in flower or not, but it does need sun and warmth to flower really well. In the average summer of a cool temperate climate, it will certainly lay down flower buds for the following spring, but a really dazzling display needs lots of sun. On the other hand, too much of this can result in a short-lived tree which flowers itself to death.

The leaves are an unusual shape, like a miniature Japanese fan, light grey-green, almost transparent, about 10 cm (4 in) wide and very nearly round with a webbing of main veins in a fan formation. Deep rosy purple pea flowers literally burst out of the branches and main trunk in mid to late spring as well as appearing more conventionally in clusters from the shoots.

Cherries

By this time the spring stage is really filling up with its cast, and mid to late spring sees the main performance of its stars, prunus (ornamental cherries). Their enemies will put them down with the dismissive remark that they 'only flower for two weeks', but it would be hard to find more beautiful flowering plants, and perhaps their fleeting quality makes them more precious, and difficult to wait for until the following spring.

Like the camellias, there are many hundreds of varieties with single, semi-double and fully double flowers, coloured white and shades of pink, crimson, purple-pink and creamy yellow. There are hybrids whose leaves are coloured in spring, and others which become brilliant in autumn. Some have a weeping habit, some are fastigiate, others are vase-shaped, or spreading and rounded to ground level. Hardy and good tempered, they do not need special conditions to flower at their best.

But the *Prunus* group also includes the ornamental plums, peaches and almonds, often much earlier flowering, in early spring. There is *P. cerasifera* 'Nigra', a pink-flowered plum, which has leaves of so deep a purple as to be almost black, remaining so throughout the season. *P. × amygdalo-persica* 'Pollardii', the single-flowered peach and almond hybrid, is deep pink and flowers at the same time, and the peach itself has pretty single flowers and probably a welcome bonus of fruit.

LATE SPRING

Crab apples

Apple trees are commonly grown for their fruit. Malus (crab apples) used to be grown far more than they are now, for the sake of the jelly that could be made from their small, tart fruits. Now it has been recognized that the 'crabs' are pretty trees in their own right, both in flower and in fruit and, because they keep to a moderate size, are among the best deciduous small trees, hardy and easily grown in most soils.

Clouds of pink, white, crimson or purplish blossom cover them in late spring; some of them have deep reddish or purplish green leaves all season. Some have brilliant leaf colouring in autumn, and all carry brightly coloured fruits in profusion – yellow, red, crimson or mixtures of reds and yellow. There is a choice of heads, too – spreading, upright or rounded, so altogether they are good value for space.

Tamarisks

Flowering at the same time but in total contrast come two more small trees: *Tamarix parviflora* (sold as *T. tetrandra*), a species of the tamarisk, and the spring-flowering species of magnolia, of which there are a number of different kinds.

Golden-leaved *Robinia pseudoacacia* 'Frisia' is a cheering sight, whatever the weather, from spring to autumn. It colours best in full sun.

The tamarisk should be much more widely grown than it is. Its minute pink flowers are gathered in fluffy clusters at the ends of the shoots all over a tree which never grows much beyond 4.5 m (15 ft) in gardens, usually less. The foliage, although deciduous, is reduced to minute, light green needle-like leaves.

Magnolias

Magnolias are sometimes called tulip trees, from the shape of their incredible flowers, though properly this name belongs to an immense and beautiful forest tree from North America called *Liriodendron tulipifera*, whose green and orange flowers are exactly tulip-shaped and sit upright on the branches. Magnolias are also American, and most of those grown in cultivation have large flowers, also carried upright on the shoots, which open from long pointed buds to a cup or bowl shape, often before the leaves. The thick petals are the variation of white which has come to be called magnolia, a matt creamy colour. *M. × soulangiana* adds a purple flush to this, on the outside of the petals, but *M. kobus* is white, mid to late spring, and so is *M. denudata*, the Yulan.

Hawthorn

If you are a bird-lover, one of the last to flower in the spring parade, lingering into early summer, is one of the best for encouraging home-loving birds. *Crataegus* (hawthorn) has a twiggy, close-knit head which provides ample nesting sites. In late spring it will be a mass of small, five-petalled flowers in creamy white, pink or rosy-red, double in some cultivars. In the single-flowered kinds these are followed by deep red or orange-red berries.

Laburnum

Last of all come the laburnums, unfortunately somewhat looked down upon as good garden trees, perhaps because they have been so widely planted. Nevertheless, their brilliant yellow waterfalls of bloom provide a display that few other plants, let alone trees, can rival, especially if the hybrid 'Vossii' is grown. It has fragrant flower clusters, 60 cm (2 ft) long.

Silver-leafed pear

Two which might just qualify for inclusion among the spring-flowering trees are *Pyrus salicifolia* 'Pendula' (weeping willow-leaved pear), and *Pittosporum tenuifolium* (New Zealand kohuhu). Strictly speaking, they do not qualify for mention here as their flowers are hidden among the foliage, which is their main reason for existence in gardens. But they do flower at this season.

CHAPTER 4

SUMMER SPLENDOUR

The summer tree scene is quite a different matter from the spring one. It can be much more exotic and lavish where gardens are warm and sheltered, and it doesn't rely so much on flowers to provide a colourful display. The leaves of some trees begin to change colour in late summer, towards the end of the season as the annual leaf-fall of the deciduous kinds comes close, and fruits change colour through the summer months into autumn so that there is always something different to look at.

One of these chameleon-like trees is especially delectable to grow – *Arbutus unedo* (strawberry tree), which carries strawberry-shaped fruits, much the same size, on the tree all year, from the time they are first formed in late autumn until the following autumn. Through the summer they hang, glowing orange and orangey red, gradually becoming deep red as they mature on a tree with dark green, leathery evergreen leaves. Cinnamon-brown, flaking bark completes the picture, provided the soil is well drained and the garden sheltered from wind, preferably near the sea.

EARLY SUMMER

Dogwoods
The cornus or cornels (dogwoods) flower at varying times of the year; one of the most architectural is *Cornus kousa*, whose branches present a striking appearance in early summer, when the white flowers are carried all along their upper sides on vertical stalks, looking like butterflies which have just landed. *C. florida* has white flowers carried quite differently, in clusters rather than regularly spaced out, all over the tree, flowering in late spring, but tipping over into early summer. The leaves of both start to change to deep red in late summer with the advance of autumn.

Cotoneaster
In early summer there are two small trees which produce masses of small creamy white flowers. Both belong to the rose family so each flower has five petals and a similar saucer shape when open. *Cotoneaster* 'Hybridus Pendulus' is a small weeping tree with the variety grafted on to the top of

a 2 m (6½ ft) stem, in time forming a dome of shoots about 2.1–2.2 m (7–7½ ft) tall.It makes a charming specimen in such small enclosed spaces as paved terraces or town gardens. It has more good qualities in its leaves which last very nearly the whole year and its deep red berries which brighten the autumn scene.

Rowan

The other species which accompanies it in flower is *Sorbus aucuparia* (rowan or mountain ash), a small tree of completely different habit. This has a rather rounded head and is a much taller tree when mature, to about 9 m (30 ft), but its height can vary a good deal, much smaller in poor soil and windy sites, where it may only be 4.5 m (15 ft), or getting on for 12 m (40 ft) where well satisfied. It is a useful tree as it is so easily grown, and is good value for space, as it flowers in summer, has striking clusters of orange-red berries in late summer and autumn, and attractive feathery leaves all through the growing season.

There are variations on it which add even more to its desirability: the

The intriguingly purple-marked white flowers of *Catalpa bignonioides*, the Indian bean tree from Carolina, are followed by long hanging pods like string beans.

Cornus florida, from the Eastern United States, is valued for its spring flowers and its bright autumn leaf colour, but the form 'Tricolor' is variegated as well.

Eucryphia glutinosa, a prolific flowering tree from Chile, is valued for its late summer season of blooming and for its upright habit of growth.

cut-leaved form 'Asplenifolia', with larger, much more sharply incised and lobed leaves, and a vertical specimen, 'Fastigiata', good where space is tight but you want to block out the neighbour's overlooking windows. There is even one with yellow berries, 'Fructuluteo', which will confuse many people who thought they knew the mountain ashes, and which apparently does the same for the birds, since they leave them strictly alone.

MID-SUMMER

Golden rain tree
A brilliantly flowered and unusual tree for mid and late summer, which loves the sun and comes from China, is *Koelreuteria paniculata*, commonly known as the golden rain tree. Showers of golden flowers in terminal clusters will cover it in hot summers especially if the previous autumn was a warm one, and the head spreads widely because the branches repeatedly fork at short spacings. The inflated bladder-like fruits which follow the flowers are large, each about 5 cm (2 in) long and nearly as wide and, together with the autumnal yellow of the leaves, continue the tree's attractiveness for several weeks.

Tamarisk
Besides the tamarisk mentioned on p. 22, there is another species, *Tamarix ramosissima* 'Rosea' (syn. *T. pentandra*), good for gardens, which begins to flower in mid to late summer, and continues until well into autumn. The flowers of this cultivar are a deep and much more decided rosy pink, produced in long plumes, rather than short clusters, at the ends of the shoots, so that a tree in full flower is a cloud of deep pink. At that time of year not only is flowering unusual, but also its colour, when so many flowers are shades of red, orange and yellow.

Magnolia
The magnolias contribute another species to summer-time with *M. grandiflora*, an evergreen kind whose large, leathery leaves are about 25 cm (10 in) long when fully grown. It grows slowly into an imposing tree with a cone-shaped head if planted in a sheltered place, and is often seen as a wall specimen facing the sun. Its fragrant white flowers open to a bowl shape 25 cm (10 in) in diameter, and appear late in summer, continuing to open in early autumn. It can grow very tall in its native southern United States, but in cool temperate climates is unlikely to be more than 9 m (30 ft). It would be difficult to better as a lawn specimen, given the right climate.

LATE SUMMER

Catalpa

If you can imagine a small version of the horse chestnut about 4.5 m (15 ft) tall and as wide, if not wider, you will have a good idea of the general size and shape of *Catalpa bignonioides* (Indian bean tree). It can grow much taller and do so very fast, but in gardens it usually stays within manageable proportions. The late summer flowers are horse-chestnut-like, too, produced in stiff upright clusters, triangular in outline, with white, bell-shaped flowers, prettily frilled at the edge, and heavily spotted purple and gold on the inside. The common name is derived from the narrow bean-like pods as much as 38 cm (15 in) long, which hang in clusters and last into winter. The heart-shaped leaves are often 38 cm (15 in) long and nearly as wide, when the tree is young.

Eucryphia

Those who are lucky enough to own a eucryphia find it difficult to wait patiently until it flowers in late summer. It is one of the loveliest and most unusual of small flowering trees when its rounded head is covered in white, bowl-shaped flowers. The centre of each is filled with a brush of yellow-tipped stamens and each flower sits framed in a cluster of leaves. *Eucryphia* × *nymansensis* 'Nymansay' is the most floriferous form of the hybrid, with flowers about 6 cm ($2\frac{1}{4}$ in) wide, lasting into early autumn. (See also p. 46).

Mulberry

As the summer goes on and autumn begins to suggest itself, many flowering trees have fruits which gradually become more conspicuous. One species whose fruits are ripe and ready for eating in late summer is *Morus nigra* (black mulberry), so called to distinguish it from the white mulberry. The former has deep crimson, almost black fruits, the latter white to pale pink berries – and the foliage preferred by silkworms. A slow-growing tree, the mulberry becomes rounded and spreading with age, on a short trunk, and often needs propping up or supporting with iron bands. A mulberry will give an air of antiquity and long establishment to a garden, and is a handsome sight when covered in its deep red fruit.

CHAPTER 5

AUTUMN AND WINTER BEAUTY

AUTUMN LEAF COLOUR

At these two seasons of the year most trees must rely on other qualities than their flowers to be decorative. The lower temperatures, even in tropical climates, do not encourage flowering, and so the trees slow their growth and may even become dormant. As a preliminary to this cessation of growth, the leaves of the deciduous species often go through a series of colour changes, turning the trees into flaming torches of red, yellow, orange and crimson.

The cornus (cornels) can be some of the most brilliantly coloured and *Sorbus aucuparia* (mountain ashes) turn to orange and yellow, as do prunus (ornamental cherries) and amelanchier (snowy mespilus). The acer (Japanese maple) called 'Osakazuki' is outstandingly red-leaved, and merits a special position, perhaps contrasted with a yellow-leaved species, or with *Pyrus salicifolia* 'Pendula' (silvery-leaved weeping pear). *Betula* 'Youngii' (white-barked silver birch) becomes a mass of golden-yellow leaves, and a group of them seen on a sunny autumn day, when the sky is blue, form a picture not easily forgotten.

The weeping cotoneaster, crataegus (hawthorns) and the eucryphia also change colour, though are less spectacular. Morus (mulberry) becomes golden-yellow leafed, as does *Koelreuteria paniculata* (golden rain tree). The good thing about all these is that they have already been decorative during spring or summer.

BEAUTY OF FOLIAGE

Foliage in general, and individual leaves in particular, tend to be overlooked in the first rush to plan a garden and make it as decorative as possible. But after some seasons, those of you who have steadily pursued planting, trying a shrub here and a climber there, designing a new border or establishing a rock garden, will begin to feel the need for plants which provide colour for as long as possible. This automatically ensures that the soil is also covered. Leaves last much longer than flowers, so why not

One of the many exquisite forms of Japanese maple, *Acer palmatum* 'Osakazuki' is richly coloured from spring to autumn, not just at the end of the season.

'John Downie' is outstanding among crab apples, since its generous crops of fruit are larger and more brightly coloured than those of other kinds – and make a lovely conserve.

choose plants primarily for the interest of their foliage, whether of shape or colour? While trees do not cover the soil closely, you can apply the same principle for decorative purposes, and choose species that are, for instance, evergreen.

The test of good garden design is its appearance in winter. It is so easy to create a charming and colourful garden during the growing season, only to be faced with a collection of empty beds in winter, filled mainly with the stick-like remains of perennials and bare soil, which invites weed growth and panned and badly drained soil – not a pretty sight from the living-room windows!

EVERGREEN TREES

The use of 'hardware' is an enormous help in improving the design of a garden – such features as paving, steps, double walls and retaining walls, arches, changes in level, arbours and so on, which give structure to the garden. A further improvement is to soften these bare bones with ever-lasting greenery – which need not be green at all. Trees are ideal for the purpose, both broad-leaved and coniferous, and the latter are particularly good in colder gardens. Their habit of growth becomes much more important, too, when they are evergreen.

Conifers

The conifers, those needle-leaved, cone-bearing trees which thrive in cold climates with heavily-snowed winters, consist mainly of evergreen species – larches are exceptions – thickly covered in foliage which often starts at ground-level. *Chamaecyparis lawsoniana* (Lawson cypresses) can be excellent 'dot ' trees, tall rather than rounded and either columnar, conical or fastigiate. Their foliage can be green, but there are some much more interesting cultivars in grey-green, blue-grey or sun-yellow. If you do want a plain all-over green, there is also *Taxus baccata* (common yew), which is dark green, with shoots held out horizontally, easily clipped to any shape you like. Female forms will have red berries. *T.b.* 'Fastigiata' (Irish yew) is naturally fastigiate, and there is a golden form of this too, good for small spaces where a spreading tree would not fit.

For a really splendid foliage colour *Picea pungens* 'Koster' (Koster's blue spruce) is one of the most electrifying. It puts all the other conifers in a collection in the shade, and is one of the most eye-catching in winter. It is a must for planting in the direct line of view from the house, and its vivid silvery-blue branches remain so all year. The habit of growth is gracefully conical.

Junipers

Juniperus (junipers) have quite different foliage, fluffy rather than spiky, but the species are also variously coloured in yellow, grey and blue-green as well as green, mostly narrowly upright and with a slow rate of growth. 'Skyrocket' is pencil slim, with blue-grey leaves, and *J. communis* 'Hibernica' (Irish juniper) is the nearest gardeners in a cool temperate climate will get to having a Mediterranean cypress (*Cupressus sempervirens*) in their garden.

Camellia/Sweet bay/Pittosporum

Camellias are planted for their glamorous flowers but they are also clothed with glossy evergreen laurel-like leaves, often to ground-level. The sweet bay is another laurel-like tree, whose leaves are much more pointed and have a matt surface. It, too, covers itself from top to bottom, as does the pittosporum, but whereas the camellia and bay are solid and chunky in their overall appearance, the pittosporum is delicately leaved in shiny light green with wiry black twigs, making a light, airy pyramid.

Hollies

A complete change in foliage shape is provided by ilex (hollies), whose prickly-edged leaves are dark green and shiny, and doubly prickly in the cultivar 'Ferox', whose upper surface is prickly too. Female forms of holly have scarlet berries, and there are kinds with yellow-edged leaves, and weeping branches, so hollies more than make up for their lack of spectacular flowers.

AUTUMN AND WINTER BEAUTY

Autumn is certainly the time for fruits, and at least a dozen of the trees mentioned in this book have ornamental berries, seed-cases and pods, in particular the ilex (hollies), crataegus (hawthorns), cotoneaster and malus (crab apples), already described. Another whose fruits are quite distinct in shape and colour from the regular run of berries is *Euonymus europaeus* (spindle tree).

Arbutus

Arbutus unedo (strawberry tree) also has dark green leaves all year, in fact manages to provide something decorative for every season. The fruit matures the autumn after it forms, changing through the year from green through yellow to its final scarlet. White flowers like those of lily of the valley open from autumn to early winter, and the bark is cinnamon coloured.

The blue spruce, *Picea pungens* 'Koster', from North America develops into a handsome, eye-catching specimen, eventually 6 m (20 ft) or more tall.

Maple/Birch

Two of the acers (maples) are also interesting for their bark. *A. griseum* has bright reddish brown bark which looks as though it has been polished, and *A. pensylvanicum* is zebra-patterned in bright light green and white. *Betula* 'Youngii' (silver birch) is another good one for winter bark colour.

Winter cherry

Winter-flowering trees are virtually non-existent, apart from *Arbutus unedo* (strawberry tree), and that is really at its best in autumn, but there is a prunus (cherry) which blooms in early winter, earlier in frost-free weather. The single white flowers on bare stems of *Prunus subhirtella* 'Autumnalis' catch the eye at a particularly incongruous time of the year.

CHAPTER 6

ALPHABETICAL DESCRIPTIVE LIST

Note: In the following descriptions, slow-growing = 23 cm (9 in) or less per year; moderate-growing = 30–38 cm (12–15 in) per year; fast-growing = 60 cm (2 ft) or more per year. If no mention is made of rate of growth, it is moderate.

Acer (maple, sycamore; family *Aceraceae*)
Acers are deciduous trees of widely varying heights, grown mainly for their leaves, which can be attractive both in colour and shape. Some also have colourful tassels of 'keys', the winged seedheads, and others have strikingly patterned and colourful bark.

A. griseum, average height 7.5 m (25 ft), can grow taller, but is slow-growing; spread about 4.5–6 m (15–20 ft); beautiful shiny bright orange-brown bark revealed as the topmost layer peels off in thin sheets; leaves, each formed of 3 leaflets, turn red or orange in autumn; central China.
A. negundo 'Variegatum', variegated box elder, 6–7.5 × 3–3.6 m (20–25 × 10–12 ft), fast-growing, graceful, spreading tree with branches down to within 90 cm (3 ft) of the ground; 3–5 leaflets to each leaf, light green irregularly margined white or sometimes completely white; tendency to revert to plain green – such shoots should be cut out completely as soon as seen; N. America.
A. pensylvanicum, 4.5–6 × 3.6–4.5 m (15–20 × 12–15 ft), snake bark maple, slow-growing; bark outstandingly striped in white and light green; leaves 3-lobed, pink as they unfold, yellow in autumn; N. America.
A. palmatum 'Atropurpureum', purple Japanese maple, 2.4–3.6 m (8–12 ft) by same spread, slow-growing; leaves narrowly 5-lobed and toothed, reddish purple all season; shelter from wind required; Japan, China and Korea.
A. p. heptalobum 'Osakazuki', 2.4–3 m (8–10 ft) by same spread, slow-growing; leaves narrowly 7-lobed, autumn colour spectacularly brilliant in shades of red and orange; neutral to alkaline soil; shelter from wind required.
A. pseudoplatanus 'Brilliantissimum', 3.6–4.5 × 2.7–3.6 m (12–15 × 9–12 ft), extremely slow-growing, 10 or 12 cm (4 or 5 in) a year only; long

buds pink, opening to pink-variegated leaves, gradually turning green; dangling tassels of 'keys', also pink; small mushroom-shaped tree when young, with much more elongated head when mature, after many years.

Cultivation. The acers are easily grown in more or less any soil, though one or two of them do better in an acid soil than an alkaline one. Sunny positions suit them best. If thinning or cutting back long stems is necessary, early winter is the appropriate season; any dead shoots or branches should be removed in early summer. Plant autumn or spring.

Increase by seeds sown in early spring or layering. Available from garden centres and shrub/tree nurseries.

Amelanchier (snowy mespilus; family *Rosaceae*)
Although not often seen in gardens, these shrubby small trees are very worthwhile growing, since they ring the changes throughout the growing season, unlike the majority of plants which have only one season of display. They are completely hardy, native to Europe, Asia, and North America where the majority of species are found. Some species grow in moist or even swampy ground, others in well-drained light soils.

A. lamarckii (syn. *A. canadensis, A. laevis*), shad bush, 3.6–6 × 3.6 m (12–20 × 12 ft), rather slow-growing with a wide-spreading head starting a few feet above the ground; leaves bronze-red in spring; white flowers about 3 cm (1 in) wide in clusters along the branches in mid spring; deep purple-black berries follow them, sweet and edible, more likely to be produced in a hot summer; leaves shades of brilliant red in autumn; North America. Its common name derives from the fact that it flowers when a North American fish called the shad goes up-river to spawn.

Cultivation. This species is the only one in general cultivation in most gardens; sun and a neutral to acid well-drained soil out of the wind will ensure the best specimens, though with good drainage and organic matter worked into the soil regularly, it will grow in a mildly alkaline one. Plant autumn to spring. Pruning is unnecessary except to thin lightly and remove dead growth – do this immediately after flowering. Increase by seed sown when ripe or by layering, suckers or hardwood cuttings, all taken in autumn. Available from larger garden centres and tree/shrub nurseries.

Arbutus unedo (strawberry tree; family *Ericaceae*)
A tree which produces strawberries seems unlikely, but in fact the fruits are extremely similar in shape and colour to the familiar summer fruit, and are edible, though rather insipid. There are several species in the genus which is mostly found in the warmer parts of Europe, the Near East and western America. Strawberry trees are most attractive and grow

wild along the west coast of southern Ireland; on the mainland of Britain they can only be grown in mild sheltered gardens, in the south and west of the country, but will withstand coastal gales there.

Arbutus unedo slowly grows to about 3 × 3 m (10 × 10 ft), more in really well-suited situations, and forks low down; bark cinnamon-brown and shredding; leaves dark green, leathery and toothed, on reddish stems; white flowers like lily of the valley, slightly scented, in clusters early autumn-early winter; orange-red, round fruit on long stalks which ripen the autumn after they first formed, so an adult tree presents an unusual and beautiful appearance for most of the year with white flowers and red fruits lighting up the dark green foliage.

Cultivation. Sun and a medium-light, well-drained soil, acid or alkaline, suit it; plant in mid autumn or late spring. Pruning is unnecessary; if tidying-up is required, do this in mid spring. Increase by seed sown when ripe; also by semi-ripe cuttings in late summer with extra heat, singly in pots, so that root-ball can be planted out intact. Available from good garden centres and shrub/tree nurseries.

Betula pendula 'Youngii' (weeping silver birch; family *Betulaceae*)
The common silver birch grows too tall, 10.5 m (35 ft) and more, to fit into the category of trees described here, but this weeping version is quite acceptable. The fine tracery of twigs, silvery white bark and diamond-shaped leaves makes it an unusual specimen tree which does not loom over and dominate the garden, cutting off the light and depleting the soil, and its shape and conspicuous bark ensure that it decorates the garden in winter. The silver birches are natives of Europe, commonly found on sandy heaths, and sometimes in swampy ground, though these are stunted, weak specimens.

Betula 'Youngii' reaches 6 × 4.5 m (20 × 12 ft); weeping branches touch the ground, making a dome shape; train the central stem up a stake to 3 m (10 ft) for the best specimens; bark silvery white, peeling; deciduous leaves diamond-shaped and toothed, on long stalks, turning bright yellow in autumn; flowers are catkins.

Cultivation. An open position and most soils except heavy ones are suitable. Birches are indifferent to the pH value, but a shallow soil over chalk will give poor results and even shallower rooting than normal. Plant any time from autumn to spring. They need strong staking in their early years. Regular training and pruning are unnecessary. Increase by layering in mid autumn. Moderately fast-growing; from garden centres and shrub/tree nurseries.

Camellia (family *Theaceae*)
Camellias are in the top class when it comes to beauty, with their large

The snowy mespilus, *Amelanchier lamarckii*, has several seasons of beauty, but its autumn leaf tints are surely the most remarkable.

and lovely flowers in pinks, reds, salmon and white, profusely produced on plants at first shrubby, and later tree-like as they become established and mature. Perfectly hardy, they are natives of China, Japan and Korea. Hybrids of *C. japonica*, the most commonly grown species, can be planted outdoors in most of Britain provided they are sheltered from cold north and east winds. Indeed, specimens festooned with icicles in winter have been known to survive and thrive in subsequent years.

They were first introduced to Europe early in the eighteenth century and were named after George Joseph Kamel, a Jesuit missionary in the Far East, who was also a plant collector and writer. The leaves of one of the species, *C. sinensis* (syn. *C. thea, Thea sinensis*), are used to provide that universal refreshment, tea, either black or green – the colour depends on whether the leaves are fermented or not during production. These evergreen shrubby trees are handsome all year round, with the peak of their attraction in spring, when their flowers last for several weeks. There are hundreds of hybrids to choose from, and the really committed 'camellian' can join a camellia society.

Camellia japonica and hybrids, 3 × 1.5 m (10 × 5 ft), but can grow much taller where suited, to 9 m (30 ft); evergreen leaves dark green, shiny, laurel-like and leathery, 10 × 5 cm (4 × 2 in); flowers 5–10 cm (2–4 in) wide, single to fully double, early-late spring depending on hybrid. *C.* × *williamsii* and hybrids, hardier, freer-flowering, with a more open and graceful growth habit, not as tall.

Camellia japonica hybrids
'Adolphe Audusson', deep red with brilliant yellow centre of stamens, sometimes white marbling on the petals, large and semi-double.
'Alba Plena', white, formal double, large, slow to grow and one of the best, early flowering.
'Contessa Lavinia Maggi', pink with red splashes, formal double, very free flowering.
'Donckelarii', dark red, marbled white, semi-double, large flowers, slow to grow.
'Mathotiana Rosea', pink, formal double, a strong-growing hybrid.
'Mercury', light red, semi-double, opening flat, very large flowers, 10 cm (4 in) wide.

C. × *williamsii* hybrids
'Anticipation', deep rose-pink with darker shadings, large, double.
'Donation', light pink, semi-double, large, profusely flowering.

Cultivation. The soil for camellias should contain plenty of organic matter, such as leafmould, peat, or rotted garden compost, and should be well-drained, medium to light, and neutral to acid in reaction. Dappled shade will give the best growth – a fully sunny place results in yellowing leaves, stunted growth and flowers falling quickly. Shelter from wind, and shade from the early morning sun are important, to prevent browning of the petal edges. Plant in mid to late spring, and water well if the weather is dry. Pruning is not required; mulch every year in spring with peat, and give a potash-high compound fertilizer dressing every year in July, watered in. Increase by semi-ripe cuttings, about 15 cm (6 in) long, with half the shoot woody, in June–July, or by layering in July–August. Widely available; particular hybrids from specialist camellia suppliers.

Catalpa bignonioides (Indian bean tree; family *Bignoniaceae*)
The Indian Bean tree has several unusual points about it which make it a good garden tree. It flowers in late summer when there is not much else in flower among the trees and shrubs, it has large soft leaves on branches which spread widely providing a good deal of shade, and it grows rapidly, but rarely becomes really tall in cultivation. Its flowers are shaped like foxgloves and, together with the long slender bean-like pods, make it one of the showier and more eye-catching ornamental trees. It is a native of eastern North America.

Catalpa bignonioides reaches about 4.5 × 4.5 m (15 × 15 ft), though it can grow taller; bark brown tinged pink; deciduous leaves heart-shaped, pale green and soft beneath, 15–25 × 7.5–20 cm (6–10 × 3–8 in); flowers in upright clusters like those of horse chestnut, each flower bell-shaped with frilled edges, white marked yellow and purple inside; mid-late summer, not produced until tree ten years old; black bean-like seedpods up to 38 cm (15 in) long in clusters hanging on tree until spring.

There is also a highly decorative golden-leaved form of this tree, of less vigorous growth but sunny from spring to autumn.

Cultivation. The Indian bean tree needs good soil drainage, but also plenty of water reserve in the soil; sun is important, together with shelter from wind, otherwise the leaves become ragged. It is unlikely to do well in the colder extremes of cool temperate climates. Plant any time in autumn or winter, and train the main stem up to about 3 m (10 ft) for the best specimens. Allow sufficient room for its spread, otherwise it will need major surgery eventually, which will spoil its shape. Increase by seed sown in spring, or by heel cuttings in summer. Available from good garden centres and shrub/tree nurseries.

Cercis siliquastrum (Judas tree; family *Leguminosae*)
The Judas tree grows wild in Southern Europe, the eastern Mediterra-

nean region and the Black Sea area, and transplants surprisingly well to southern Britain. It is chiefly grown for its flowers, but also has pretty, rounded leaves, and large, conspicuous coloured seedpods from mid-summer. Legend has it that it was the tree on which Judas hanged himself. Introduced to Britain at the end of the sixteenth century or early in the next one, the Judas tree may owe its introduction both to its ornamental qualities and to the fact that the flowers could be eaten, and were added to salads or fried in butter together with the young buds.

Cercis siliquastrum grows to about 3–4.5 m × 2.4–3 m (10–15 × 8–10 ft); deciduous grey-green leaves, round with fan-like veins, produced in late spring two or three weeks after the flowers; flowers deep pink-purple early in late spring, pea-like, thickly produced in clusters all along the bare shoots, and directly out of the branches and trunk; pods large and flat, 10 cm (4 in) long, starting out purple but changing to brown later in autumn.

Cultivation. Well-drained soil and a hot, sunny position are ideal; heavy soil and chilly, windy sites are quite unsuitable, but given warmth and sun, the Judas tree will thrive and be one of the prettiest of small trees for the garden. It dislikes being transplanted, so plant from a container and choose a plant less than 60 cm (2 ft) tall; plant in mid spring or early autumn. If there are two or three main stems, cut out two of them and train the remaining one to a stake. There is no need to prune. Increase by seed sown when ripe in a propagator. Available from better garden centres and shrub/tree nurseries.

Chamaecyparis (kam-e-sy-par-is) (cypress; family *Cupressaceae*)
The cypresses are part of the group of trees called conifers with evergreen resinous leaves, often needle-like, and cone-shaped, woody 'flowers'. Lawson cypresses provide a variety of foliage colour such as grey, blue-grey, dark and light green, yellow, and variegated white or yellow. The leaves consist of flattened sprays of scale-like leaves, somewhat fan-like. Their dense growth makes them ideal for providing shelter and privacy, and the colourful and attractive shape, together with the pyramidal or columnar growth habit ensure that they are among the most useful and decorative garden trees – never more so than in winter. North America.

C. lawsoniana 'Columnaris', slowly growing to 6–7.5 m (20–25 ft) but only about 90–120 cm (3–4 ft) wide, columnar, blue-grey, lovely specimen in a lawn.

C. l. 'Fletcheri', slow-growing to 7.5–9 m (25–30 ft), by 1.8–2.4 m (6–8 ft), broadly conical, grey-green feathery foliage.

Catalpa trees are characterized by their unusually large heart-shaped leaves. The golden form, 'Aurea', best in full sun, is especially decorative.

C. l. 'Lanei', slow-growing to 7.5 m (25 ft) or more, 1.2–1.5 m (4–5 ft) wide, columnar, golden-yellow feathery foliage all year.

C. l. 'Pembury Blue', 6–7.5 m × 1.8–2.4 m (20–25 × 6–8 ft), pyramidal, young leaves blue-grey, becoming green from second year, so that a mixture of blue-grey and green is always apparent on the tree.

Cultivation. Lawson cypresses are not demanding as to site or soil, though a heavy soil and/or a lot of chalk are unlikely to produce the best specimens. Deep moist but well-drained soil can produce some excellent specimens. Plant in early-mid autumn or mid spring; do not prune unless to shape or remove dead growth, then do this in early-mid spring. Increase by 7.5 cm (3 in) long heel cuttings in late summer, put into sandy compost in a covered propagator. Widely available.

Cornus (cornel, dogwood; family *Cornaceae*)
A group of mostly deciduous trees and shrubs, among which are the shrubby dogwoods, whose flowers, bark and leaves are all attractive at different times of year. There are three species of trees in the genus which

A mature Judas tree, *Cercis siliquastrum*, is smothered in rich pink pea flowers in spring, just before its leaves appear.

fit well into smaller gardens, and which are hardy and easily grown. This is not surprising since the shrubby *Cornus sanguinea* (dogwood) is native to northern Europe, and most of the species are found in temperate parts of the world. The common name dogwood is derived from *dag*, a spike or skewer, and the generic name from the Latin *corneus*, horny, a reference to the texture of the wood.

C. florida, 3–6 m (10–20 ft) and 3 m (10 ft) wide; leaves to 15 cm (6 in) long and half as wide, becoming brilliantly orange and red in autumn; white petal-like bracts about 5 cm (2 in) long surround the tiny flowers and appear in late spring in clusters; there is a shorter variety *rubra* whose bracts are pinkish red, flowering in early summer. Eastern USA.

C. kousa, 3–6 m (10–20 ft), but usually not more than about 3 m (10 ft), wide-spreading to about 2.4 m (8 ft); branches tabulate; the variety *chinensis* has bigger flowers; leaves oval and pointed, with strongly marked parallel veins, as in all the cornels, turning deep red in autumn; 'flowers' consist of four conspicuous white pointed bracts with the true and insignificant flower in the centre. Japan, Korea, China.

C. mas, Cornelian cherry, slowly growing to about 4.5 m (15 ft), with a densely twiggy head; oval pointed leaves to at least 10 cm (4 in) long; flowers bright yellow, small, produced in tufts in late winter and early spring on the bare stems, before the leaves appear, an enchanting sight when the bare branches are wreathed in yellow, especially as they appear in winter; fruit bright red, rounded, edible and pleasantly sharp. Europe.

Cultivation. All these small trees are hardy and will grow in most reasonable soils and situations; however, *C. kousa* is at its most vigorous in a peaty soil, and both it and *C. florida* flower at their best in sun. *C. mas* will thrive in dry soils. None of them needs pruning; increase is by seed sown when ripe, or by layering, if there are any shoots near enough to the ground. Available from better garden centres and specialist tree/shrub nurseries.

Cotoneaster (family *Rosaceae*)

There are times when, although a tree is called for, it should be a really small one. That is not to say that it should be shrubby – it still needs to be tree-like, with a single main stem, topped by a bushy head. But the final height should be only about 2.1 m (7 ft) to ensure that it is in proportion to its surroundings, which might be a patio, a small paved town garden, a basement area or a roof garden. Or it could be a feature by a stream or a small pool.

For such surroundings, there is a cotoneaster which is ideal, *C.* 'Hybridus Pendulus'. Normally cotoneasters are shrubby, though some are much larger than one would expect, up to 3 m (10 ft) and as much wide, but this hybrid is grafted on to a 1.8-m (6-ft) trunk, from the top of which it trails weeping branches, eventually down to ground level, making a dome about 1.2–1.5 m (4–5 ft) wide, with a mature height of about 2.1 m (7 ft). The dark shiny leaves are semi-evergreen, and in some warm and sheltered positions will be completely evergreen. In early summer each shoot is a rope of creamy white flowers and, since the bees find them irresistible, they are soon replaced by brilliant red berries right down to the tips of the stems, often lasting well into winter. Origin unknown.

Cultivation. Cultivation is easy. They are not fussy about soil or position provided the standard soil preparation is carried out, and need no pruning unless an aberrant shoot is growing vertically or too fast downwards at the expense of the others. Treatment for it can be in early spring. Available from shrub/tree nurseries and good garden centres.

Crataegus (hawthorn, may; family *Rosaceae*)

The deciduous thorns provide a good deal of shade with their wide-spreading, dense heads, and are grown for their flowers and, in some cases, fruits and autumn colouring. They are good bird-encouragers, since their twiggy growth offers ideal nesting sites, and there is food to follow in autumn. Rate of growth for those described below is about 45 cm (1½ ft) a year, though *C. prunifolia* is slower, at less than 30 cm (1 ft) annually – and they are extremely hardy.

C. monogyna (the 'quick' of British hedgerows) is often seen as a small tree covered in a cloud of white blossom in fields or at the sides of hedges, where it has seeded from its hedge parents; 6–7.5 m (20–25 ft) with the same spread; dark green 3- or 5-lobed leaves 4 cm (1½ in) long, creamy white single flowers late spring, deep red berries autumn; Europe.

C. × lavallei 'Carrierei' (syn. *C. carrierei*), about 4.5 × 3.6 m (15 × 12 ft); large, deep green leaves up to 11 cm (4½ in) long; large white flowers an inch wide in early summer; large, orangey red berries which are actually not liked by birds and last all winter; France.

C. oxyacantha 'Paul's Scarlet', Paul's scarlet thorn; the deep red flowers are tight little double rosettes in clusters covering the tree. *C. o.* 'Punicea Flore Pleno', rosy pink flowers, also double. Height and spread of both are about the same at 4.5 × 3.6 m (15 × 12 ft); both flower late in late spring and early summer, but berries are few and far between; European trees.

C. prunifolia, the plum-leaved thorn; about 6 × 7.5 cm (20 × 25 ft), branches often reaching down to ground level, so allow it room to do this; 9 cm (3½ in) long leaves, oval, dark green and toothed but without the lobes usually seen on hawthorn leaves, changing to crimson in autumn; single white flowers early summer, followed by deep red fruit, falling in autumn. Origin unknown.

Cultivation. There are no problems about cultivation; most sites and soils, provided they are not waterlogged, will suit them. Indeed, the thorns can be used as nurse trees in seaside gardens to provide shelter for less gale-proof plants to get a foothold. Pruning is unnecessary except to thin or tidy in early spring. Increase by seed stratified for 18 months and then sown in spring, or by grafting. Available from shrub/tree nurseries and most garden centres.

Eucryphia (family *Eucryphiaceae*)

The eucryphias must be amongst the top ten of the prettiest flowering small trees in the world. If your garden is suitable, it would be a pity not to plant one – it forms a striking lawn specimen and has the added advantage of flowering at an unusual time of year.

When its display of large white flowers has become but a memory, *Cornus florida* surprises us with a brilliant display of leaf colour.

Eucryphia glutinosa, the hardiest species, growing slowly to 4.5–6 m (15–20 ft) and almost as much wide; in warm gardens it is almost evergreen, i.e. its leaves hang on until mid winter; leaves consist of several leaflets in pairs forming a fern-like shape, turn red and yellow in autumn if they are going to fall; saucer-shaped white flowers mid-late summer, nearly 7 cm (3 in) wide with a prominent brush of long yellow-tipped stamens in the centre, slightly scented, can easily cover the whole tree; Chile.

E. × *nymansensis*, evergreen, grows slowly to 7.5 m (25 ft) tall, more in conditions which suit it, and about 6 m (20 ft) wide; has *E. glutinosa* as one parent, and *E. cordifolia* as the other; leaves are fern-like or have the simple, oblong shape of *E. cordifolia*, which donates their everlasting quality; white flowers, not as large as those of *E. glutinosa*, opening later in late summer; origin Sussex, England, though both parents come from Chile.

Cultivation. Eucryphias need sun to flower, so should be planted in an open space where they will get all the sun going. Unhappily they are not for colder areas in cool temperate climates, but in the south and west of such areas, with shelter from wind, will develop into delightful small specimen trees. Soil needs to be well-drained, acid in reaction for *E. glutinosa*, and with plenty of humus in it; *E. × nymansensis* will grow in alkaline soil. Mid spring planting is best, and it is advisable to protect young trees in the first few years after planting from late autumn until early spring, and to mulch them for the winter.

There is no need for regular formal pruning, but a little of the oldest growth, together with weak shoots, can be removed in early spring. Increase is not particularly easy, though seed sown in spring in pots of peat-based compost can be tried, planting out the following spring; note that it takes more than a year to ripen, so allow for this before sowing. Autumn layering is also possible, together with 7-cm (3-in) long cuttings of sideshoots taken in midsummer and given warmed compost. Rate of growth about 23–30 cm (9–12 in) a year. Available from shrub nurseries.

Euonymus (spindle-tree; family *Celastraceae*)
William Turner, born in the sixteenth century, who is said to be the father of botany, remarked when describing this tree that the Dutch name for it meant spindle – apparently in Holland the wood was used for making spindles for weaving. It was also once used for making the stems of pipes, skewers and toothpicks.

The spindle is mostly found growing wild in hedges and light woodland in Europe and, with cultivation, will grow into a small tree about 6 m (20 ft) tall and perhaps 2.4 m (8 ft) wide. It is deciduous; the trunk and branches are bright green, and although the leaves and small greenish yellow flowers are nondescript, the clusters of 4-lobed fruit are quite dazzling, with their bright rose-pink skins splitting to show the brilliant orange-coated seeds inside. *E. europaeus* is the wild species, and there is a good cultivar of it called 'Red Cascade', much smaller and slower growing, but regularly weighed down with larger, red-pink fruit, a magnificent sight in autumn and early winter. The leaves often form a crimson background to them before they fall in autumn.

Cultivation. There are no problems with cultivation. Any reasonable site and soil will suit spindle-trees, and the only pruning that need be done is in the first few years, cutting away surplus shoots low down to ensure a clean main stem free from side growths. Increase by seed sown in spring.

Growth moderate, about 30–38 cm (12–15 in) annually. Availability widespread for the species; 'Red Cascade' from shrub/tree nurseries and the larger garden centres.

Fraxinus excelsior 'Pendula' (weeping ash; family *Oleaceae*)
Unbelievable though it may seem, the ash is a member of the same family as the Mediterranean olive and the Indian jasmine. But of course it has to be remembered that plant classification is based on the flowers and the parts which make them up, not on the leaves, habit of growth, hardiness, fruits and so on, as one might think.

The common ash can grow 42 m (140 ft) tall, but the height of the weeping form will depend on the point on the main trunk at which it is grafted. It can be 7.5 m (25 ft) tall, or it can be considerably less, and if you are prepared to order, and do so sufficiently far in advance, you should be able to specify the final height. A weeping ash will hang right down to the ground and form a hollow dome, a natural arbour in fact, providing shade from the sun, shelter from wind and a 'cave' for children to play in, as well as being a striking specimen tree for a lawn.

Its weeping habit is its raison d'être; the fern-like leaves 30 cm (1 ft) long cover it from spring to autumn, but the tiny flowers are without petals and the 'keys', or winged seeds, have no special merit.

Cultivation. The weeping ash is perfectly hardy and not particular as to site or soil; special care is not necessary, and pruning need only remove the occasional vertical shoot. Rate of growth is about 45–60 cm (1½–2 ft) while young, slowing down with maturity. Available from shrub nurseries and some garden centres, but may need to be ordered from the latter.

Ilex (holly; family *Aquifoliaceae*)
There are species of holly native to almost all parts of the world, but the one perhaps best known to gardeners is *I. aquifolium*, native to Europe and western Asia. Its associations with midwinter festivals lie in the fact that it was a symbol of eternal life and had many medicinal uses. It brought good luck for the year if used to decorate a house over Christmas, but if it was taken down before Twelfth Night the good luck was thrown away. Prickly-leaved holly was thought to be masculine, smooth-leaved had a feminine ambience, but in fact these qualities depend on the sex of the flowers of each species or variety. All hollies are evergreen.

Each tree may have either all-male flowers or all-female ones. Only the latter will have berries, so you mostly need two trees to be sure of berries on one, unless there is a male form growing nearby, perhaps wild. However, there are a few self-fertile hollies which are described on p. 49.

Ilex aquifolium, common holly, 24 m (80 ft) tall in the wild, in cultivation about 6 m (12 ft) and about 2.4–2.7 m (8–9 ft) wide; it is slow-growing at about 23 cm (9 in) a year, less if variegated-leaved. Glossy, dark green, leathery leaves cover the plant fairly densely, providing a good wind shield, and privacy all year; prickly except for the leaves near the top; tiny white flowers late spring; bright red berries autumn and winter.

Female forms: *I. a.* 'Argentea Marginata', irregular white edges to the leaves; 'Mme Briot', yellow margins and mottling in the centre of the leaves, as well as purple-black bark on the young shoots; *pendula*, weeping with plain green leaves, and 'Argentea Pendula', white-margined leaves; *I.* × *altaclarensis* 'Golden King' smooth, yellow-margined leaves; all with scarlet berries, provided they have a mate.

Male forms: *I. aquifolium* 'Silver Queen', white-edged leaves marbled in the centre, with purple bark on young shoots; 'Ferox', the hedgehog holly, prickles on the surface of the leaves as well as at the edges, and its white- and yellow-edged forms 'Ferox Argentea' and 'Ferox Aurea', and finally 'Golden Queen', with wide yellow edges.

Self fertile: *I. aquifolium* 'J. C. van Thol' (syn. *I. a. polycarpa*), plain green leaves, not very prickly, and a sport from it with yellow-edged leaves, 'Golden van Thol'. *I. a. heterophylla* 'Pyramidalis', plain green with leaves both toothed and entire; both kinds berry profusely.

Cultivation. The common holly and the Highclere (× *altaclarensis*) holly are easily suited as to soil and site, being indifferent to sun or shade and satisfied with any soil provided it is not permanently wet. However, it should be noted that the climate of the north-eastern states of America does not encourage the best growth, and here the native species *I. opaca* and its varieties should be substituted.

Plant in early to mid autumn or in mid spring if there is a choice, and prune in mid spring if tidying is needed, or the trunk needs clearing of sideshoots; sometimes plain-leaved shoots appear on variegated trees – these should be cut out completely as soon as seen. Increase by ripe seed stratified in sand; even so, germination will take at least 18 months. Increase also by semi-ripe heel cuttings of sideshoots in late summer placed in an unheated propagator. Widely available from shrub nurseries and garden centres, though selection of varieties will vary from supplier to supplier.

Juniperus (juniper; family *Cupressaceae*)
The evergreen junipers are conifers like the cypresses, and can be particularly useful to gardeners as they will grow well on chalk, where the evergreen tree heaths and tree rhododendrons will not. Their dense, rather feathery foliage can be variously coloured; shapes also vary. The berries

are yellow (male) or green (female) but gradually turn blue-black over a period of two-three years as they ripen. It is these berries that are used to flavour Geneva or Dutch gin and liqueurs; they are also used as a spice for meat, particularly game. Most juniper species are shrubby or prostrate, but some are tree-like, albeit slow-growing, with elegant shapes.

J. chinensis 'Aurea', Young's golden juniper, slow-growing, a few inches a year, forming a broad column-shaped tree 9 m (30 ft) high after many years, and half as wide at the base; young foliage golden in its first season, clothing tree to ground level; China, Japan and Mongolia.

J. communis 'Hibernica', Irish juniper, about 3 m (10 ft) tall on average, though can be taller, and 75 cm (2½ ft) wide, slow-growing, forms a dense narrow column much like a small Italian cypress; silvery grey foliage; origin uncertain.

J. c. suecica, Swedish juniper, about 2 m (6½ ft) after ten years, and 60 cm (2 ft) wide, tapered to the top; blue-green foliage, shoots slightly drooping at the tips – there are two clones and this is the best one, the other is much more pyramidal and shrub-like; northern Europe.

J. scopulorum 'Blue Heaven', pyramidal, 4.5 × 3 m (15 × 10 ft), slow growing, 15 cm (6 in) a year; very blue-green foliage, making it a distinctive and attractive specimen tree; western North America.

J. virginiana 'Skyrocket', narrow and pencil-like, 4.5 × 60 cm (15 × 2 ft), rate of growth about 30 cm (1 ft) annually, slowing down with maturity; blue-grey foliage; one of the most striking of the columnar conifers and excellent for restricted spaces; east and central North America.

Cultivation. Sunny positions and moist but well-drained soil suit junipers best; they will grow quite happily on alkaline soils, including those containing chalk. Best planting times are mid–late spring and early–mid autumn; any shaping needed should be done in mid spring. Increase by 7.5-cm (3-in) long heel cuttings Aug–Sept., in sandy compost and an unheated propagator; also by seed sown when ripe – germination can take a year, and seedlings will vary from parent. Available from shrub/tree nurseries and some garden centres.

Koelreuteria paniculata (golden rain tree, family *Sapindaceae*)
This tree only just qualifies for inclusion in this book, but it can be such an ornamental tree, at a time of the year when many plants are past their most ornamental, that it is worth describing. In its native habitat of China height can be 18 m (60 ft), but it can also be only 9 m (30 ft), and in cool temperate climates such as Britain and northern Europe, it rarely

reaches 7.5 m (25 ft). An average height is much more likely to be 4.5 m (15 ft), and the spread appears to be rather variable – some forms are tall and narrow, others are wide-spreading. Rate of growth about 30 cm 12 in) a year when young.

The golden rain tree has feathery or pinnate leaves, rather like those of the mountain ash, but with the leaflets much more markedly toothed; in autumn they turn brilliant yellow before they fall. Flowering starts in mid summer and continues into late summer, with golden flowers in terminal clusters nearly 30 cm (12 in) long, rather like a yellow wisteria. The fruit forms an inflated pink bladder about 5 cm (2 in) long, with a dark brown, pea-like seed inside each.

Cultivation. As much sun as possible ensures the best flowering, together with shelter from wind and a well-drained soil; severely cold winters are likely to kill it. Plant in autumn or early spring. Pruning is not necessary. Increase by ripe seed sown in early spring or by root cuttings taken in late winter and given artificial warmth. Available from specialist shrub and tree nurseries.

Laburnum (family *Leguminosae*)

Although laburnums are so easily grown, and stand up to severely cold winters, they are natives of central and southern Europe, where they grow in the mountains. They were one of the earliest trees to be introduced to cultivation in Britain, in 1560, and have been grown in gardens ever since. Exceptionally pretty small trees, they are ideal in every respect, *except* that all parts are poisonous, especially the seeds.

Laburnum alpinum, Scotch laburnum, 6 × 3 cm (20 × 10 ft), deciduous leaves divided into three leaflets; bright yellow scented flowers in hanging clusters up to 25 cm long in early summer; will grow in moist soils.
L. anagyroides, (syn. *L. vulgare*) common laburnum, 7.5–9 m (25–30 ft) tall by about 3.6–4.5 m (12–15 ft) wide; leaves in three parts; yellow flowers in late spring, in clusters 15–20 cm (6–8 in) long; withstands drought better than the Scotch form; there is a cultivar 'Pendula', with long drooping branches.
L. × *watereri* 'Vossii', a hybrid between the two species described, height and spread as for *L. alpinum*, scented yellow flowers in hanging chains up to 60 cm (2 ft) long, early summer; seeds much less prolifically.

Cultivation. Any reasonable site and soil will suit laburnums; they will be at their best on medium to light soils, and chalk is not a problem. Plant between autumn and spring, and don't worry if they take a long time to come into leaf after planting – they may not do so until midsummer, but in the meanwhile will have been developing roots and establishing beneath the soil. Staking is important while young as they are readily blown into a permanent slant by the wind. Prune only to remove suckers. Increase by seed sown when ripe in a cold frame, or by grafting. Rate of growth 30–38 cm (12–15 in) annually. Widely available.

Laurus nobilis (sweet bay; family *Lauraceae*)

The bay leaves of cooking are taken from this tree, an evergreen, rather bushy species covered in leaves down to ground level, forming a pyramidal specimen, handsome all year round. Its leaves were those used in the crowns of winners of ancient Greek athletic events, and the tree was once dedicated to Apollo; later, sprays of leaves and flowers formed the wreaths for the poet laureate. Now the leaves chiefly have use in food, particularly as an essential ingredient for bouquet garni, and are used commercially to flavour liqueurs.

Laurus nobilis grows to 4.5–6 × 1.8–2.4 m (15–20 × 6–8 ft), much taller in its native Mediterranean habitat, and has dark green, leathery leaves, generally entire and aromatic. It flowers quite freely in cool temperate climates when grown in a sunny place, the small, creamy white flowers being produced during late spring in clusters in the leaf joints nearest the light. Rounded black-purple berries follow them, about 1.5 cm wide.

Cultivation. Most soils, provided they are well-drained, suit it, and a sunny, sheltered position will produce the tallest and most floriferous specimens. Once established, it is hardy, though the leaves will be browned in severely cold winters, but when young it needs protection. Plant in early-mid autumn or mid spring, and protect from cold wind all winter, and from prolonged frost by covering entire plant. Prune to shape by clipping in mid spring. Increase by half-ripe cuttings taken in late summer in a frame with heated compost, or by layering in late summer-early autumn. Rate of growth about 23 cm (9 in) a year. Widely available. When buying plants, examine them closely for the presence of scale insect – once present, it is extremely difficult for gardeners to eradicate it, and so it is better not to buy plants which are infected.

Magnolia (family *Magnoliaceae*)

The magnolias are highly desirable flowering trees and shrubs from eastern Asia and the United States; many are tropical, but nearly as many are native to temperate climates. Their outstanding characteristic is their flowering ability; the flowers are mostly large, tulip-shaped in bud, and open to globular or saucer-like blossoms, carried upright on the branches. An adult tree in full flower is a magnificent sight, and a plantation of them would make an outstanding feature.

Some are evergreen, some deciduous, some flower early, some in late summer – some are heavily scented. For such exotic-looking trees to be hardy is rare, and if conditions in the garden are right, they should not be difficult to grow.

Magnolia grandiflora, evergreen, to 7.5–9 m (25–30 ft), pyramidal and about 2.4–3 m (8–10 ft) wide at its widest, moderately slow-growing, about 23 cm (9 in) annually; roughly oblong leaves 25 cm (10 in) long, leathery and dark green with a reddish brown felt on the underside; creamy white, thick-petalled globular flowers up to 25 cm (10 in) wide when open, strongly fragrant, late summer-autumn, produced on trees from the age of eight years, provided they were grown from cuttings or layers; southern United States.

M. kobus, deciduous, to about 9 × 3 m (30 × 10 ft), forming a pyramid when young but later becoming round-headed, quicker-growing than other magnolias at about 45 cm ($1\frac{1}{2}$ ft) a year; oblong leaves up to 15 cm (6 in) long; white flowers in profusion, 10 cm (4 in) wide with rather star-shaped petals, mid spring; pink-tinged fruit; age at which it flowers is variable, from eight–twelve years, earliest if vegetatively propagated; Japan.

M. denudata, the Yulan, deciduous, to 6–7.5 m (20–25 ft) with a rounded head about 2.4–3 m (8–10 ft) wide (taller in its native country); oval leaves to 15 cm (6 in) long; white cup-shaped flowers 15 cm (6 in) long, early to late spring, depending on weather; flowering is best when winter is consistently cold or consistently mild; the Yulan is one of the prettiest of the magnolias; China.

M. × soulangiana, deciduous, to 3.6–4.5 m (12–15 ft) by the same width, forming a tree with a short trunk as it matures, but shrub-like while young; oblong leaves 15 cm (6 in) long; fleshy-petalled flowers tulip-shaped, at least 10 cm (4 in) long, white on the inside, purple flushed on the outside, mid spring, before the leaves, but continuing until the end of late spring (the form 'Lennei' has even better flowers but is more of a shrub); hybrid origin, from France.

Cultivation. The magnolias flower best in a sunny place sheltered from wind, not in a frost pocket – frost and wind will both brown the flower petals and may even result in the buds staying closed; soil should contain plenty of humus in the form of leafmould or peat, and should be deep and well-drained. Hot light soils, whether sandy, shingly or chalky, are unsuitable – those with a neutral to acid reaction are preferred, though slightly alkaline ones with a good humus content will be acceptable.

Magnolias have fleshy roots, which rot when injured; plant in late spring when growth has started and the plant can more easily develop

Magnolia blossoms, particularly those of *M.* × *soulangiana*, the most widely planted kind, are a highlight of spring gardens. We all wait to see if they escape browning by frost or cold winds.

Small weeping trees are valued for their graceful shape and compact size. This is the crab apple, *Malus* 'Echtermeyer' (syn. *Malus* × *purpurea* 'Pendula').

new roots to take the place of the injured ones, and heal the injuries. Take particular care with planting, spreading the roots right out if bare-rooted, and using plenty of peat or leafmould; water in well and mulch deeply.

Pruning is unnecessary; protect from severe cold in winter while young. Increase by semi-hardwood cuttings in late summer placed in a heated frame, or by ripe seed cleaned of its sticky outer coating, sown in a frame – expect it to take one to two years to germinate. Rate of growth 15–30 cm (6–12 in) a year; availability mainly shrub and tree nurseries, and the larger garden centres.

Malus (ornamental crab apple; family *Rosaceae*)
The apples are perfectly hardy, deciduous trees more often grown for their edible fruits. But there is a group containing the crab apples which, small and rather acid though they are, can nevertheless be turned into delicious jelly. The flowers of these are even more decorative than those of the orchard hybrids, and there is a choice between white, pink, purple or crimson blossom; some have a bonus of coloured foliage, and most have colourful fruits as well. Easily grown and long-lived, they form one of the best groups of small trees. Temperate regions of the Northern Hemisphere.

Malus 'Golden Hornet', 4.5–6 × 4.5 m (15–20 × 15 ft), upright growing while young, later with a spreading head; white flowers and bright yellow, pear-shaped fruit lasting on the tree until early winter.
M. 'John Downie', 6–7.5 × 4.5 m (20–25 × 15 ft), pink-budded white flowers in late spring, conical fruit more than an inch long, brilliant yellow to orange, flushed red, heavy crops, particularly good for jelly.
M. 'Profusion', 4.5 × 3.6 m (15 × 12 ft), more spreading head than 'Golden Hornet' and 'John Downie', young leaves purple, later brownish green; flowers heavily in deep crimson; small fruit deep red, about 1.3 cm ($\frac{1}{2}$ in) wide.
M. × *purpurea*, 4.5–6 × 4.5 (15–20 × 15 ft), broad-headed and arching with maturity; leaves purplish red when young, later purple-flushed green; flowers crimson, in mid spring; fruit deep red and round, about 2 cm ($\frac{3}{4}$ in) wide.
M. 'Red Jade', 6 × 4.5 m (20 × 15 ft), white flowers late spring; fruit deep red, shiny, round, 2.5 cm (1 in) wide, lasting most of winter.
M. *tschonoskii*, taller than these hybrids, 7–9 × 2.1–3 m (25–30 × 7–10 ft), pyramidal habit; leaves grey-felted when young and brilliant mixture of colours in autumn–red, orange, purple and brown, making a striking display; flowers white, flushed pink, 3 cm ($1\frac{1}{4}$ in) wide; fruit round and purple-brown but rarely produced.

Cultivation. Any soil, unless really badly drained or extremely alkaline/acid, will grow good crab apples, and choice of aspect and site are equally wide ranging. Plant autumn–spring, and prune only to shape, to thin or to remove diseased shoots and branches; do this in winter and, if mildew is a problem, remove mildewed shoots as soon as seen, in late spring. However, crab apples are more resistant to diseases than the orchard kinds, and are unlikely to be infected with either this or scab; canker of the branches is most likely, in badly drained soil and areas of high rainfall. Cut out and dress wounds with wound-sealing compound. Increase by grafting in early spring. Rate of growth 45–60 cm ($1\frac{1}{2}$–2 ft) annually.

Morus nigra (mulberry; family *Moraceae*)
The black mulberry forms a pleasantly rounded, spreading tree forking low down in most cases, so that the trunk is quite short, 60–90 cm (2–3 ft). It is one of the longest cultivated tree species, for thousands of years – so long in fact that it is only known to come from somewhere in western Asia. Its cultivation has been mainly due to its edible fruit, but its leaves serve a purpose, too, as they are food for the silkworm – not the main source of supply for these larvae, however, as they prefer the leaves of the white mulberry, *M. alba*. Unfortunately, when James II of England tried to start a silk industry in Britain, he arranged for the import of the wrong species, and the British countryside is still littered with gnarled specimens of black mulberries left over from the original plantings of the late 1600s. Whenever you see a really old mulberry, even if it is in a town garden, it is likely to be one of these, and there was probably a large garden there originally, or even a small plantation of mulberries.

The black mulberry reaches about 7.5–9 m (25–30 ft) eventually, but slowly, and often only about 4.5 m (15 ft), when its spread is even greater. The deciduous leaves are heart shaped with a pointed tip, sometimes lobed and 7.5–23 cm (3–9 in) long; the nondescript flowers are in short spikes in late spring, to be followed by fruit like large raspberries, deep wine-purple coloured when ripe in late summer, and staining readily. May be eaten raw, otherwise cooked or made into jam.

Cultivation. Plant in a sunny place and a medium to heavy but well-drained soil in late autumn or early spring; leave the roots untouched as far as possible, as they are fleshy, and plant with particular care. Formal pruning is not required and cutting of the shoots or branches should be avoided as far as possible as the wood 'bleeds', even in winter. If it does, check it with ashes. Increase easily by cuttings or even branches 30 cm (1 ft) long in early-mid autumn outdoors. Rate of growth 30 cm (1 ft) annually, less when mature; available from shrub and tree nurseries and the larger garden centres.

Picea (spruce; family *Pinaceae*)
Most of the species of spruce are much too big to be described here. This means that, unless you are particularly keen, or are prepared to dig it up when it grows too large, the Christmas tree, *P. abies*, cannot be included in your collection of small trees.

However, there are two cultivars of *P. pungens*, the Colorado or blue spruce, which do not grow too tall or too fast, and are extremely ornamental as to foliage all year. They make some of the most ornamental lawn specimens.

P. pungens 'Hoopsii', 6–7.5 × 2.4–3 m (20–25 × 8–10 ft), but often only 4.5 × 2.1 m (15 × 7 ft); dense habit, foliage light silvery blue, needles short, about 2.5 cm (1 in) long; cylindrical cones about 7.5 cm (3 in) long, green to yellowish brown.

P. pungens 'Koster' ('Koster's Blue'), 6–7.5 × 2.4–3 m (20–25 × 8–10 ft), but likely to be much less in many gardens; forms a pyramidal habit with branches produced in tiers at regular intervals; foliage intense blue-grey; needles and cones similar to 'Hoopsii'.

Cultivation. Spruces will do best in deep, moist but well-drained soils, but will also grow reasonably well in wet, cold ones; dry, shallow or chalky soil is not suitable. Any sunny or open site provided it is not windswept, is acceptable. Plant in mid autumn or mid spring; there is no need to prune. Watch for aphids; there is one which is specific to spruce and can cause bad defoliation. Increase by grafting on to seedlings in early spring, or by heel cuttings in late summer in sandy compost and an unheated frame. Cuttings are not easy to root because of the resin contained in the tissue, but this can be reduced if cuttings are dipped in hot water for two or three minutes. Rate of growth about 20 cm (8 in) a year; available from shrub and tree nurseries or specialist conifer suppliers.

Pinus (pine; family *Pinaceae*)

Unfortunately practically all the pines are large forest trees; few are dwarf and shrub-like. If you would like a smallish tree-like pine the least tall are around 12–15 m (40–50 ft), and thus do not qualify for the small tree category which mainly falls in the 4.5–7.5-m (15–25-ft) range.

Pittosporum (parchment bark; family *Pittosporaceae*)

The peculiar name of these small, sometimes shrub-like evergreen trees, refers to the seeds; the Greek *pitta*, pitch, and *spora*, seed, indicate that the seed has a sticky outer layer, due to resin. Pittosporums have graceful, rather airy shoots and delicate, light grey-green leaves, which can clothe them down to ground level. As they are evergreen, this makes them unusually attractive and, although the tree species most easily grown in cool temperate climates comes from New Zealand, it is hardy in all but the severest winters, provided it has a protective fence or wall.

P. tenuifolium, (kohuhu), tree to 9 m (30 ft) tall and forming a head 4.5 m (15 ft) wide in the wild, in positions that suit it well; often only 3.6 or 4.5 m (12 or 15 ft) tall; leaves oblong or ovate with undulating margins, light green and shiny, carried on twiggy growth, black when young; fragrant flowers deep purple with yellow anthers, small trumpet-shaped 1.3 cm ($\frac{1}{2}$ in) long, late spring, produced profusely after sunny summers.

P. t. 'Garnettii', slightly less tall, but wider; white-margined leaves, tinged pink in winter, not as long as those of *P. tenuifolium*.

Cultivation. The species is surprisingly hardy, the variegated form less so, but even so will not survive a severely cold winter, and should be given shelter from wind and a sunny position to ensure the most decorative appearance. Otherwise the shoot tips will be browned and, if the leaves are exposed to a continuous easterly wind in winter, defoliation and death will follow. But periods of short frost will not do great harm to an established tree growing in well-drained soil. Plant in mid-late spring; prune only to maintain a good shape and to thin in mid spring. Increase by semi-hardwood cuttings in late summer placed in warmed compost in a propagator, or by ripe seeds sown in spring under cover. Rate of growth, about 15–23 cm (6–9 in) a year; available from shrub and tree nurseries, and some garden centres.

Prunus (ornamental cherry, plum, peach, almond; family *Rosaceae*)
Flowering cherries are unique in the loveliness of their blossom; there are no other small flowering trees in the same class, and whatever size your garden is, it should contain at least one flowering cherry. The difficulty comes in choosing – there are so many that cover themselves in clouds of blossom, white, shades of pink and red or yellow.

The Japanese varieties are the cream of the group, having been grown in Japan for at least 1500 years. They were first planted by a Buddhist priest, who brought them from China, at the time Buddhism was introduced to Japan, and have been grown there ever since, though they did not reach Europe until the middle of the 19th century. Flowering cherries are also widely grown today in China.

Besides the cherries, there are also ornamental plums, almonds and peaches, each of which has its own attractions. These are completely hardy, like the cherries; in cool-, warm-temperate and sub-tropical zones they will grow satisfactorily, but in tropical regions they do not do well, as they need a period of cold, particularly plums.

Below is a short list of species, hybrids and cultivars, but it is only a selection from a vast list. If you have the time, it would be worth obtaining the catalogue of a specialist shrub and tree nurseryman giving details of many more.

P. × *amygdalo-persica* 'Pollardii', hybrid between peach and almond, about 6 × 5.4 m (20 × 15 ft), head rounded; leaves pointed and deeply toothed; flowers single, deep pink, 5 cm (2 in) wide, early spring; fruits have a bitter kernel.

P. cerasifera 'Nigra', ornamental cherry plum, 6–7.5 m (20–25 ft) with a spreading head of the same measurement; black-purple leaves; single, deep pink flowers profusely produced in early-mid spring.

P. 'Cheal's Weeping Cherry', height 1.8–2.1 × 3 m (6–7 × 10 ft), forms a dome with branches weeping down to ground level; double, deep pink flowers wreathe the branches all along their length, late in mid spring.

P. 'Erecta' (syn. 'Ama-no-gawa'), very narrow, upright growth, eventually 6 m (20 ft) tall, but width only about 60 cm (2 ft); flowers profusely, semi-double pink, slightly fragrant flowers, mid-late spring; sometimes sets small black cherries.

P. incisa (the Fuji cherry) 4.5–6 m (15–20 ft), rather bushy when young and as wide as its height, but later elongating, rounded head with a width about two-thirds of its height; leaves deeply toothed and long-pointed; flowers so profusely as to cover the branches, pink-budded, single flowers opening white, early in mid spring; black fruit.

P. 'Kanzan', vase-shaped habit, about 7.5 × 9 m (25 × 30 ft); young leaves bronze, changing to yellow, brown and orange in autumn; flowers double, purplish rose-pink, late in mid spring.

P. padus 'Watereri' (syn. *P. p.* 'Grandiflora') (bird cherry); pyramidal habit, 6–9 × 6–7.5 m (20–30 × 20–25 ft); leaves up to 12.5 cm (5 in) long; small, white, fragrant flowers in spikes up to 20 cm (8 in) long, late spring and early summer; although not tall-growing, it needs quite a lot of space to spread sideways.

P. 'Pandora', 6–7.5 × 2.4 m (20–25 × 8 ft), vase–shaped, more spreading when mature; leaves bronze when young, shades of red and purple in autumn; flowers single, shell-pink, early-mid spring.

P. persica 'Klara Mayer', 6 × 4.5 m (20 × 15 ft), spreading head; flowers deep pink, double, mid spring (no fruit because it is double-flowered).

P. 'Pink Perfection', 7.5 × 7.5 m (25 × 25 ft); leaves pale bronze-green when young; flowers double, reddish in bud, deep pink when open, 5 cm (2 in) wide, mid-late spring.

P. 'Shimidsu' (syn. *P. serrulata longipes*), 4.5 × 4.5–6 m (15 × 15–20 ft), rounded head, somewhat weeping when mature, almost to ground level; young leaves pale bronze-green, red and orange in autumn; flowers in clusters on stems up to 17.5 cm (7 in) long, pink in bud, opening white, semi-double, 5 cm (2 in) wide, late spring, exceptionally pretty.

P. 'Shirotae', 6 × 6–7.5 m (20 × 20–25 ft), flat-topped habit with branches in tiers; leaves large and light green, later yellow in autumn; flowers white, fragrant, single to semi-double, 5 cm (2 in) wide, mid spring, profusely produced on branches which can be down to ground level; particularly good as a lawn specimen.

P. subhirtella 'Autumnalis', 7.5–9 × 7.5 m (25–30 × 25 ft), rounded head; leaves brown, red and orange in autumn; flowers pinkish, opening to white, single, usually on bare branches from late autumn, but in early seasons at the same time as the coloured leaves, making a distinctively attractive display, continue to open during mild spells in winter until leaves reappear in spring, slightly fragrant; there is a form called *P. s.* 'Autumnalis Rosea', with deep pink flowers.

P. 'Ukon', 6 × 7.5 m (20 × 25 ft), vase-shaped with short trunk, ultimately lowest branches arching over to ground level; leaves bronze when young, red, orange, brown and wine in autumn; flowers primrose-yellow, semi-double, 4.5 cm ($1\frac{3}{4}$ in) wide, profusely produced, and making an attractive combination with the bronze-coloured young leaves, mid-late spring; grows more quickly than other cherries.

Cultivation. Cherries will grow well in most situations with shelter from north and north-east wind; prefer a deep loam soil containing lime, and if there is none present, chalk or some other form of lime should be mixed in some weeks before planting, preferably in summer. Plant any time in autumn or winter; if pruning is required, do so sparingly, as the shoots or branches tend to 'bleed', and will need to be treated with a protective wound-sealing compound. Cut out crossing or crowded shoots, also those damaged, dead or diseased, so that light can get into the tree and ripen the shoots well; any pruning should be done in late summer.

Bacterial canker, peach leaf curl, blackfly and caterpillars are the most likely troubles. The symptoms of bacterial canker are brown spots on the leaves, followed by tiny round 'shot-holes' in the leaves in spring as the brown areas drop out, and the leaves turn yellow and fall; there may also be gumming of the shoots and branches, and on the main trunk, and whole shoots or branches can die back, with death, eventually, of the entire tree. Cut out dead or badly damaged growth in late summer and cover wounds with a fungicidal sealing compound. Spray in spring with Bordeaux mixture, also in late summer, the beginning of early autumn, and in mid autumn, to provide a protective covering. Note, however, that this fungicide can burn the leaves badly and must be applied with care, and never in windy conditions.

Peach leaf curl infects the leaves as they unfold from the dormant buds, so that they develop thickened yellow areas looking like blisters, later turning red, with a blue bloom on the surface. The affected leaves fall early and with infections in successive years, the trees become weak and stunted. Infection is most likely during cold wet springs. Spray with Bordeaux mixture when the leaf buds are swelling in late winter or early spring, and repeat as the leaves start to fall in autumn, with another application as soon as leaf fall has finished. The object is to protect the buds when the fungus spores become active and infective, and to prevent further infection through the wounds left by the falling leaves. Infected leaves should be collected as soon as seen and destroyed.

Increase by grafting in early spring, or by budding in mid summer; also by the stone if available, though the seedling will not be true to its parent; for *P. incisa* try semi-hardwood cuttings in mid summer, in a propagator. Rate of growth in general is 30–45 cm (1–1½ ft) annually; widely available, but apply to specialist tree and shrub nurseries if a particular variety is not stocked by a local garden centre.

Pyrus (pear; family *Rosaceae*)

The fruiting pears are the varieties mainly grown in the temperate climate zones of the world, cropping most heavily where summers are warmest and rainfall is moderate. Although they can be covered in white blossom in mid spring — a truly magnificent sight — they are not otherwise ornamental. However, there is no reason why they should not be grown for ornament, with the bonus of a good crop of edible fruit later – they are not by any means the only variety of small tree to have just one season of beauty.

But there is an ornamental species of pear, called *P. salicifolia*, which grows slowly to a height of about 7.5–9 m (25–30 ft), more in sheltered situations, with a head taller than broad, 3.6–4.5 m (12–15 ft) wide. The shoots tend to hang down, and the whole head of the tree forms a rather tangled mass of silver-grey. The deciduous leaves are willow-shaped, as the name suggests, that is, narrow and pointed, and coloured almost white due to the down on them. Soon after flowering this disappears, and the leaves become grey-green. In mid to late spring, masses of single white flowers appear, nearly an inch wide, lasting two or three weeks, followed by small, pear-shaped inedible brown fruits.

There is a cultivar, called *P. s.* 'Pendula', slow-growing, to about 6 × 3.6 m (20 × 12 ft), and much more weeping, down to ground level, forming a dome shape. This is even more attractive and ideal for restricted spaces, or as a container tree. It is often used to provide a splash of silver to relieve the ubiquitous green or hot colours.

Cultivation. Most sites and soils will suit it, with the best flowering occurring in a sunny place. Plant autumn or early spring. There is no need to prune, except to remove dead, broken or diseased growth and this can be done in winter. Increase by budding in mid summer or grafting in early spring. Cuttings could be tried in summer or autumn, depending on whether they are semi-hardwood or hardwood. Rate of growth 23–40 cm (9–12 in) annually; available from the more specialist garden centres, and shrub and tree nurseries.

Robinia pseudoacacia (false acacia, locust; family *Leguminosae*)
This species of robinia grows into much too large a tree to be included in the small-tree category, which is a pity, as its branches are gracefully held and clothed with pretty feathery leaves and white flowers. But it has a cultivar, found in a Dutch nursery before the Second World War, which contains its growth and is a delightful and unusual specimen tree. The species is native to North America.

Robinia pseudoacacia 'Frisia' matures at about 7.5–9 m (25–30 ft) tall, depending on the soil and position, with a head which is long rather than spreading, about 4.5 cm (15 ft) wide. It is as graceful and attractive a tree as its parent. The leaves are a brilliant golden-yellow as they unfold and, unlike many yellow-foliaged plants, remain yellow all season until autumn, when the colour does finally pale and become tinted with pale orange before the leaves fall. 'Frisia' also has hanging clusters, up to 17 cm (7 in) long, of white pea flowers in early-midsummer, fragrant enough to perfume the air surrounding them.

Cultivation. 'Frisia' can be planted in sun or dappled shade, and is easily grown in most soils, even sandy ones which are short of water. But it is advisable to choose a site which is well protected from wind, as the shoots and branches are very brittle. The shoots will constantly snap off in a windy position, making mowing a lawn a problem, and the branches of mature trees will also break readily, so shelter is important. Plant in autumn.

Regular pruning is not necessary, but as it grows fast when young, cutting back the leading shoots in the early years by perhaps a quarter in early winter will help it to strengthen its growth, thus minimizing the possibility of breaking, and to bush out more. Increase by suckers, or by grafting in spring on the parent species.

Salix (willow; family *Salicaceae*)
The willow family is a large one, and contains hundreds of species and varieties, found throughout the Northern Hemisphere, from tropical to polar regions. It is also a widely varying family in its habit of growth. The large weeping willow grown beside pools and lakes is well known, but shrubs, small trees, and tiny prostrate creeping species are forms also found in it. Its ease of growth and the weeping habit of some varieties make it popular, but there are also species whose catkin-like flowers are attractive and eye-catching.

The narrow, pointed leaves are considered typical of the willow species, and plants in other genera, whose leaves are the same shape, are often specifically called *salicifolia*, but in fact there are a considerable number of willows with rounded leaves, sometimes semi-evergreen if the species is a tropical one.

The golden weeping willow referred to above is a beautiful tree, but grows much too large to be described here, up to at least 18 × 9 m (60 × 30 ft), and is, unhappily, quite unsuitable for the size of many of the gardens in which it is planted. However, there are other weeping willows which are smaller.

Salix caprea 'Kilmarnock' (syn. *S. c.* 'Pendula'), weeping form of the goat or pussy willow — also called sallow or palm — naturally weeping, umbrella-shaped, down to ground level, about 4.5 m (15 ft) tall in time, and 3 m (10 ft) wide, leaves round to narrow and pointed; separate male and female forms, with male catkins about 2.5 cm (1 in) long, softly and silkily grey-furred, covered in yellow anthers, and female catkins twice the length, less decorative than the male, early-mid spring on bare branches; Scotland.

S. matsudana 'Tortuosa' (dragon's claw willow) non-weeping, in the wild about 12 m (40 ft) tall, but in cultivation only about 7.5 m (25 ft) with a spread of 3.6 m (12 ft); remarkable for the contorted and corkscrew-like twigs and branches, particularly in winter when bare of leaves and silhouetted against the sky; willow-like leaves similarly twisted and curved; slow-growing after about 10 years; will grow well in dry soils; North China.

S. purpurea 'Pendula', weeping, mushroom-shaped form, to ground level 3.6–4.5 × 3 m (12–15 × 10 ft) wide, bark on young growth purple; leaves narrow and pointed, blue-green or silvery green on the under-surface; grafted on to a main stem about 2.4 m (8 ft) tall, grows 38 cm (15 in) a year, less when mature; Europe, North Africa, Asia.

Cultivation. Willows nearly all have the highly desirable characteristic of needing moist soil in which to grow, and will survive winter waterlogging, and even summer soil moisture for that matter; the weeping cultivars described here are no exception. Sun or shade are immaterial, though sun will give the best growth and the most profuse display of catkins; planting can be any time from autumn to spring. Regular pruning is unnecessary, but some cutting back may be required if shoots on the weeping forms are showing a tendency to become vertical; damaged or diseased growth can be removed at the same time, during winter.

Willows, especially the commonly planted large weeping variety, are prone to a fungal disease called willow anthracnose, symptoms being dieback of the tips of the shoots, small red-brown spots on the leaves, and canker on the stems — cracking the overlying skin or bark – all of which spread rapidly in spring.

Salix purpurea 'Pendula' is the most likely of these three to be infected, but even so, will largely escape the disease. If it does occur, control it by cutting out infected growth back to healthy tissue as soon as seen, and spraying with Bordeaux mixture every three weeks from the time the buds start to unfold until early in mid summer, to maintain a complete protective cover; do not spray if the temperature is high. The disease is worst in wet springs and summers.

Increase by hardwood cuttings taken in autumn and inserted outdoors. Rate of growth 30–60 cm (1–2 ft) annually when young, less with maturity. Available from larger garden centres and shrub and tree nurseries.

Sorbus (rowan or mountain ash, whitebeam; family *Rosaceae*)
The mountain ashes and whitebeams are hardy, deciduous trees found growing throughout the Northern Hemisphere, mostly in mountainous areas and damp to wet soils. Mountain ashes in particular are typical of the Scottish landscape. The genus only just qualifies for inclusion in small trees, since some of the species have a minimum height of 9 m (30 ft), but of course they will not necessarily always grow to that height — soil and climate can easily limit them to 6 m (20 ft) or less. Some of the cultivars and hybrids are, in any case, naturally much smaller. Their chief attraction lies in the colour of the fruit, but some also have good foliage, finishing with autumn colouring.

Sorbus aria (whitebeam) 9 × 6 m (30 × 20 ft), taller in good soil, spreading head; leaves almost round, up to 10 cm (4 in) long, toothed and with thick white felting on the underside; flowers creamy white, in stiff clusters 7.5 cm (3 in) wide, late spring; round, scarlet berries. Europe, except Scandinavia. *S. a.* 'Chrysophylla', similar to above but less tall, and with yellow leaves all season, long rather than rounded. *S. a.* 'Lutescens', as its parent, but more cone-shaped growth habit; leaves when young and unfolding are silvery grey on both sides and stand up straight, so that the whole tree seems to be covered in candles — a most attractive and unusual sight. Later the foliage is greyish green on the upper side, and in late summer, the leaves at the shoot tips have a yellowish tinge.
S. aucuparia (mountain ash or rowan) minimum height 9 m (30 ft) with a rounded head one-third to half as wide; leaves fern-like up to 23 cm (9 in) long, with about seven pairs of leaflets; tiny white flowers in clusters late spring–early summer; orange-red berries autumn and early winter; Europe and Asia.
S. a. 'Asplenifolia', as above, but with deeply indented, toothed leaflets, and less tall-growing; a more graceful tree.
S. a. 'Fastigiata', completely vertical growth until well matured, then

The whitebeam, *Sorbus aria* 'Majestica', cousin to the mountain ashes, yields clusters of scarlet fruits in autumn against a background of golden leaf tints.

tending to spread a little, a good tree for limited horizontal space; height as *S. aucuparia*, but leaves longer, and fruit deep crimson, much more profusely produced.

S. a. 'Fructuluteo', (syn. *S. a.* 'Xanthocarpa'), as its parent, but smaller, to 6–7.5 × 3–4.5 m (20–25 × 10–15 ft), and with yellow berries.

S. cashmiriana, 7.5–9 × 4.5–6 m (25–30 × 15–20 ft), loosely spreading head; leaves feathery and toothed, up to 16 cm (6½ in) long; flowers white with a pink tint, 1.3 cm (½ in) wide, much larger than usual, and in clusters as much as 18 cm (7 in) wide, in late spring; berries 1.3 cm ($\frac{1}{2}$ in) wide, also in clusters, white with fleshy, pink-tinted sepals, lasting well into winter; western Himalaya.

S. vilmorinii, 7.5 × 6 m (25 × 20 ft), spreading head; leaves to 15 cm (6 in) long, feathery with leaflets in as many as 14 pairs, dark green, becoming red and orange in autumn; flowers small and white in loose clusters in late spring; fruit a flattened globe, deep pink, to white with maturity; an unusual tree, more decorative than most, but unfortunately rarely grown and seldom seen; north-west China.

Cultivation. There are no problems with the mountain ashes or the white-beams; they will grow in most sites and soils and do not object to wind. If there is any possibility of choice, the whitebeams thrive in alkaline soils, the rowans in neutral or acid ones. The rowans do not like prolonged heat or drought. Plant autumn–winter, and prune, in winter, only for shaping or removal of damaged or diseased growth. Increase by grafting in spring, or the species by seed sown, after stratification, in a cold frame or propagator, in spring. Rate of growth 30–60 cm (1–2 ft) annually; widely available in varieties from specialist tree/shrub nurseries.

Tamarix (tamarisk; family *Tamaricaceae*)

Pretty feathery trees, the tamarisks are small and bushy, found in cool temperate to tropical regions everywhere except the New World. They often grow wild beside the sea, in sandy soil, even in sand dunes.

T. ramosissima 'Rosea' (syn. *T. pentandra*), 3.6–4.5 × 3.6 m (12–15 × 12 ft), spreading head arching over towards the ground; tiny, light green leaves, narrow and 3 mm ($\frac{1}{8}$ in) long, crowded on the shoots to give a plume-like effect; flowers pink, equally tiny, in long feathery clusters at the ends of shoots covering the tree, from mid summer–early autumn. 'Pink Cascade' has much deeper pink flowers, and is strong-growing, producing 1.8 m (6 ft) of growth in a season.

T. parviflora, similar but the clusters of flowers are shorter to about 7 or 10 cm (3 or 4 in), and are produced in late spring on shoots which grew the previous summer. It is usually sold as a form, under the name of *T. tetrandra*, and is not native to salty soils.

Cultivation. Tamarisks are easily grown, being particularly suited to coastal gardens and dry soils; windy sites present no problems. Where the soil is deep and moist, they tend to become over-vigorous at the expense of the flowers; a sunny position will always encourage better flowering. Plant in late autumn or early spring. Pruning will greatly improve flowering and *T. ramosissima* should be cut back hard in spring, to encourage good new growth on which the summer's flowers will be carried; leave only a few inches of stem from which new shoots can sprout. Prune *T. parviflora* as soon as flowering has finished in spring, but less hard, so as to remove about one third the length of flowered shoots, and thin where crowded. If preferred, the trees can be left alone, and will still flower. Increase by hardwood cuttings in late autumn outdoors. Fast-growing, widely available.

Taxus (yew; family *Taxaceae*)

The yews were once considered to be conifers, but botanists now regard them as forming a separate order. They do not produce cones or carry seeds in them, but form a fleshy colourful fruit (aril) in which the seed is enclosed. Yews are hardy, evergreen trees, found throughout the temperate regions of the Northern Hemisphere, and in Britain large areas were once covered in woods composed mainly of yews; their great use was for making bows before guns became the main weapons of war. For modern garden use, their dense, dark green foliage is windproof, and decorative, and their hardiness and the permanent nature of their leaves make them even more of a good choice. There are also varieties with golden leaves. The bark, leaves and fruits of the yew are poisonous, so it should not be planted where livestock can reach it.

T. bacccata (common yew) 9 × 9 m (30 × 30 ft), can be more; narrow, dark green leaves 1.3 cm ($\frac{1}{2}$ in) long, virtually in pairs clothing the shoots; male flowers a cluster of stamens, females near the end of the shoots forming a small, densely packed cluster of leaf-like bracts surrounding the ovule, males and females on separate trees; fruit bright red, fleshy with a hard round seed inside it.
T. b. 'Fastigiata', Irish yew, vertical habit with several upright branches from a single trunk, 9 × 2.4 m (30 × 8 ft).
T. b. 'Fastigiata Aurea', leaves golden-yellow, slower-growing than the green-leaved form.
T. b. 'Fastigiata Aureomarginata', leaves yellow-edged, male only.

Cultivation. Any aspect, sunny or shady, sheltered or windswept, can be used, together with most soils including those containing chalk, though avoid really badly drained ones. Plant autumn–early winter or mid–late spring. Pruning unnecessary, but yew is easily shaped, if required, by cutting in mid to late summer. If it needs rejuvenating, late spring is the best time to do it. Increase by seed sown when ripe, or by 10–15 cm (4–6 in) long cuttings of semi-ripe shoots taken in mid to late summer and put in sandy compost in a propagator. Slow-growing when mature, but while young extends by about 30 cm (1 ft) a year. Widely available in the common form, varieties from specialist nurseries.

CHAPTER 7

OBTAINING TREES

Trees are the longest-lived of plants, and so money is well spent on one which has been carefully chosen to suit its site, as well as for its decorative qualities, and which is in the best of health from the start.

THE TREE FOR THE SITE

It is not exaggerating to say that it is a matter of life or death to fit the tree to its site, to make certain that the soil suits its needs, that it will receive the light or shade it requires, and has shelter from wind or protection from cold. Buying a tree is an investment which can pay high interest for many years. Choosing the wrong kind for the conditions your garden offers can defeat this objective completely from the start, though it may take two or three years before it becomes apparent that the tree is not going to thrive or even survive.

HEALTH OF THE CHOSEN TREE

Given that the species is suitable in the first place, it is then important to choose a healthy specimen. In an ideal world, there would be no question of this and, to be fair, the standard of plant health in nurseries and garden centres is usually high. Nevertheless, keep an eye open for splits in the bark on the main stem, cracking due to cankers on branches as well as trunks, broken branches and shoots, poor colour of green leaves, insect pests such as aphids on the shoots and leaves, or scale insect on the bark – and also the under surface of leaves, particularly on the sweet bay.

SHAPE
Look for a well-shaped tree. One which has much more growth on one side of the trunk than the other, or which has one shoot growing much more strongly than the remainder, or which is lopsided in some way, will be difficult to straighten up by pruning. A crooked trunk is unlikely ever to become properly vertical. Weeping forms should be symmetrical and hang down evenly all round the trunk. If they do have an aberrant shoot starting to grow vertically, this is not such a problem as it would be on a

conventionally shaped tree, as it can be cut off flush with its point of origin without upsetting the rest of the naturally weeping growth. Badly balanced growth can also occur in containerized trees if they have not been planted centrally, so that the roots develop more on one side than another.

TREES FROM GARDEN CENTRES

It is not always realized that two different species of trees sold for roughly the same price can be quite different in size. For instance, a 2.1 m (7 ft) crab apple can be the same price, or even less, than a winter-flowering cherry, perhaps only 1.5 m (5 ft) tall. This may be because of its rarity value, the difficulties of propagating it, or slowness of growth.

There are two main sources for obtaining trees: garden centres and mail-order nurseries (which sometimes have a garden centre attached). You can also buy trees from DIY outlets, which nearly always have a small gardening department, though the range is greatly restricted. It is a good idea to check before a visit that they have any trees at all.

Fig. 1 Slit the black plastic container in which the tree has been grown down two sides before removing it to avoid disturbing its ball of soil and roots. Otherwise its re-establishment could be delayed.

Fig. 2 Cut back any dead or damaged roots to healthy tissue so they do not offer a foothold to fungus diseases.

Garden centres vary a good deal in their standards of plant quality and selection. If both are good, they will very often supply a descriptive price-list of plants in stock. If you do have a good garden centre nearby, it is probably better to buy your trees from it, as you can see what is available and make your own choice. You can also ensure that its shape is exactly as you would like it. You will then have only yourself to blame if it is a poor specimen!

Trees in garden centres are nearly always grown and sold in containers, which does undoubtedly have its drawbacks. Trees are slower to sell than other plants, and may remain in their containers too long. Even with adequate feeding, the roots will become cramped and distorted and, for a potentially long-lived plant, this is much more serious than it is for perennials or shrubs. Such trees can of course be planted immediately (Fig. 1), even in summer, provided they are regularly and thoroughly watered in hot dry weather, but it is difficult to be sure in advance that they are not root-bound, without asking an assistant to remove the container.

If you do buy from a garden centre, there could also be a problem in getting a 2.1 or 2.4 m (7 or 8 ft) tree home in the car. Trees which are several years old will be several feet taller still.

MAIL-ORDER NURSERIES

Trees from mail-order nurseries overcome this difficulty at the cost of a post and packing charge, but delivery is usually restricted to the autumn, winter and early spring, particularly if they are bare-rooted (Fig. 2). This means that they are grown in the open ground, then dug up and the roots cleaned completely of soil before they are packed in moist peat or straw and wrapped in polythene sheet. Although the roots are broken by this method, it is mainly the anchor roots, and the fine feeding roots nearer the surface are hardly damaged. Provided the latter do not become dry between lifting and replanting, there should not be any serious problem.

It is advisable to place a mail order several months in advance of the traditional planting time to ensure that it arrives when you want it to. Late autumn–early winter is generally the best time to plant, but evergreens can be exceptions. Look in the A–Z list for the right time. If the order arrives when the soil is unfortunately frozen, waterlogged or covered in snow, undo the top of the wrapping and allow the tree light and room to breathe and expand its shoots and branches, but leave the roots as they are, in their moistened packing material, and protect from frost.

If the weather is still difficult after three or four days, put the tree in a container of compost, again kept frost-free, or try to find a corner which is sheltered and not too wet or cold, and heel it in (Fig. 3).

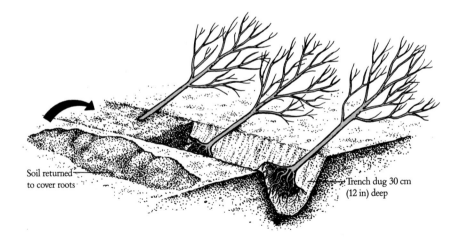

Soil returned to cover roots

Trench dug 30 cm (12 in) deep

Fig. 3 If unable to plant trees straight into their permanent positions because the soil or weather is not fit or you have not time, heel them in to keep their roots moist. Bury their roots in a shallow trench, leaning the trees at a low angle.

CHAPTER 8

STARTING WITH TREES

Once you have decided what shape and size of tree you want, and what its colouring should be, whether of leaf, flower or berry, its hardiness should be considered, together with the choice of site and soil. These practical aspects are more important with trees than any other garden plants. If you are successful in placing it, the result will be not only a healthy and ornamental tree, but a long-lived one, giving pleasure for half a century or more. Conversely, if you plant it in the wrong place, it will be some time, perhaps two, three or more years before it shows signs of real distress, and by then it will be too late to dig it up and try it somewhere else, and those years will have been wasted.

CHOOSING A SITE

Practically any tree will be satisfied with a south, west, or east-facing aspect; a northerly one is best planted with the hardier trees. Whatever the aspect, shelter from wind, especially the prevailing one, will result in a sturdier and taller tree, flowering well and fruiting better – pollinating insects dislike working blossom in windy condition.

Planted in the line of the prevailing wind, a tree will inevitably be shaped by it, and may even be stunted. Planted where it receives the full winter blast of the northerlies or easterlies, it will have to be very hardy to survive undamaged. In coastal gardens the wind, although strong, is not quite such a problem, as the climate is milder, but salt carried in the wind can cause trouble in summer gales. It is common to see the leaves of trees browned on the side facing the wind after this kind of 'blow', and the foliage may even be completely torn off, but this appears to do no great lasting damage.

Sunny sites, backed by other larger trees, woodland or thickets of large shrubs, can be reserved for the more delicate species, and for those with particularly beautiful flowers – the camellias, eucryphias and magnolias are examples; the Judas tree is a sun-lover and so, too, is the golden rain tree, *Koelreuteria paniculata*.

Frost pockets – areas where the cold air pours down a slope, just as water would, and collects at the bottom because there is a fence or other barrier in the way – should be avoided where flowers or berries are the main features. Magnolias often finish up spoilt by browned petals or even with unopened buds due to icy cold nights – and sometimes days. If the centres of flowers are caught and blackened by frost, as for instance those of the crab apples, there will not be any decorative fruit to follow.

TYPE OF SOIL

Choice of soil is just as important, too. Fortunately there are few trees which will not grow in alkaline soil, but be sure that you know what reaction your soil gives to a test to ascertain whether it is acid or alkaline. The acid-loving ones will die fairly rapidly in alkaline soils.

Some trees prefer moist deep soils, others need dryish light ones. Most of them prefer good drainage, though it is surprising how well they will survive bad drainage, particularly the hardier varieties. If a prolonged period of very wet weather occurs, even this will do little damage, provided they are well-rooted, and have been established for some years. But a permanently high water-table should be reserved for those trees which grow naturally in such conditions, such as willows. Any exceptions to this should again be the hardiest species – hawthorn or the spindle-tree – but this is still risky.

You can determine pretty well what kind of soil you have by feel. Those which allow the water to pour through them, feel gritty, and it is difficult to make a fistful stick together, even when wet. They can still be dug easily after heavy rain; the soil will not stick to fork or spade and they quickly need copious watering during hot sunny weather. Chalky soil will drain easily as well and will be light-coloured, sometimes with lumps of chalk in it; seaside garden soil will often have shingle in it as well as sand.

Water-retaining soil is distinctly sticky and glutinous when wet. Its critics compare it with plasticine or putty, and it is unfortunately true that clay subsoil can be worked between the fingers in much the same way and, smoothed out, makes an excellent and waterproof lining to a pool. This was actually the way in which ponds were sometimes made in the old days, with straw or bracken acting as a base first on to which the clay was layered. Not surprisingly, after heavy rain, a hole dug in clay soil will retain water at the bottom for some hours, and if roots are subject to such waterlogging for many weeks or months, they will eventually die, due to lack of oxygen in the soil, and the build-up of root secretions and the residues of decaying soil flora and fauna to toxic proportions in the soil water.

When preparing soil for planting, extremes of both these conditions can be alleviated by adding rotted organic matter, such as garden compost, farm manure, spent mushroom compost, peat or leafmould. In light soil it will help to retain water and bind the soil particles together; in heavy soil it will separate it and introduce air spaces. In both cases, the humus and nutrients it contains will encourage the presence and activity of other soil inhabitants, and this in turn will result in further improvements in soil structure and texture.

SOIL PREPARATION

The site for planting should be dug and cleared from weeds about a month in advance. Two spades' depth is not too deep, and an area of 60 cm (2 ft) square about right. Fork up the base of the hole, mix in organic matter and return the soil also with this material mixed with it. Try to make sure that the top-soil goes back last, in its original place. Use about half as much organic matter as there is soil.

If there are perennial weeds present, and you have the time, dig them out thoroughly several months in advance, and then go on removing the new shoots which inevitably appear from pieces of root overlooked earlier. Alternatively use a weedkiller such as glyphosate which affects the weed plant through the top growth and so does not contaminate the soil, and repeat if necessary. Then you will be sure not to have the much more difficult problem of clearing the weed once the tree is planted.

In well broken-down heavy soil, good loam or newly dug grassland, there will not be any need for a fertilizer dressing, but light soil, long-worked old garden soil, peaty soil and those containing chalk should have their food content improved by forking a balanced compound fertilizer into the soil before planting. Bonemeal, which contains phosphorus, is quite good, and will go on being useful for several years afterwards, but a compound dressing will supply nitrogen and potassium as well, the other two most important nutrients, and blood-fish-and-bonemeal can be used, or an 'artificial' i.e. not organic, fertilizer such as Growmore. The organic ones take longer to have an effect, but last longer. Rates of application are in the region of 112 g/sq m (4 oz/sq yd), but look to see what the manufacturers direct on the container.

PLANTING TECHNIQUE

Plant when the soil is moist, but not when sodden, frozen or dry. Dig out a hole sufficiently deep to take the roots spread out if bare-rooted, or to take the root-ball if container-grown or 'balled'. Drive in a supporting stake, whether single, or double with a cross-bar, before putting the plant in the hole, at least 30 cm (1 ft) deep, preferably more, ensuring that its top comes just below the head if the tree is a standard or half standard.

For bare-rooted plants, cut any broken roots back cleanly, and any which are much longer than the others back to manageable proportions, then put the tree in the hole so that the soil-mark on the stem is level with the soil surface. Crumble the soil back in over the roots, shaking the tree as you go to settle the soil, and tread it at intervals. A gardener's mate to hold the tree while you do this is a great help. When the hole is full, tread down the soil, add more if necessary to level it, firm again and rake. Then mulch with a bulky organic, keeping it clear of the base of the stem (Fig. 4).

If the trees are planted in a lawn or other grassed area, keep an area at least 60 cm (2 ft) square clear round each one for the first five years or so,

Fig. 4 Planting a bare-rooted tree
(a) Dig out a hole of suitable depth and diameter to take the tree's roots, then hammer in a stake before planting.
(b) Position the tree in the hole close to the stake and spread out its roots. A board laid across the hole acts as a guide to planting level.
(c) Return the soil gradually, shaking the tree gently up and down to settle soil around its roots.

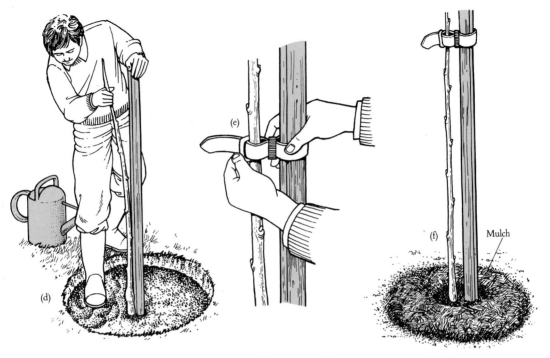

(d) Fill the hole in stages, firming the soil with your boot as you proceed. Then water in generously.

(e) Secure the tree to its stake with a tree tie.

(f) Finally, mulch the soil round the tree to keep its roots cool and moist. Keep the trunk clear of mulch so mice are not encouraged to nest and gnaw the bark.

again to cut down competition for nutrients and moisture. The better start the tree has, the stronger it will be when mature.

Container-grown plants should be removed carefully from the container – cut it down one side first – and placed in the hole without disturbance beyond cutting any long coiled roots at the base. Balled plants are freed of their covering if it is plastic sheet or netting, but not if it is sacking. For both, the soil is filled in round the sides mixed with an equal amount of potting compost, and firmed in well to the same consistency as that of the root-ball, finishing off with organic matter as before. In dry weather water in well, and repeat every other evening until rain occurs. Conifers should be further treated by spraying their top growth daily with water. Mulch as when planting bare-rooted trees, and protect all with tree guards.

CHAPTER 9

CARING FOR TREES

The care that is needed for trees immediately after they are planted depends on whether they have been planted while dormant, between late autumn and early spring, or while growing, during spring and summer – and the earlier autumn months. There is also a considerable difference in the way they are treated if they are evergreen rather than deciduous trees.

AFTERCARE IN WINTER

For those planted during autumn and winter, the need will be to make sure they are secure and are not wind-rocked. If their supports are unstable, or if the trees themselves have not been planted firmly enough, the trunk will whip to and fro repeatedly in winter gales so that a cup-shaped hollow forms at soil-level round the base. This will fill up with water and can lead to infection by fungus diseases and a rapid death of the young tree.

If such hollows do form, fill them with soil well firmed down, drive in the support more firmly and re-tie the tree. Ensure that the soil is really well tamped down; frost is another hazard leading to raised and loosened soil.

Once trees are well established and as they mature, heavy snow can result in broken branches. In one respect snow is beneficial, as it provides a blanket protecting them from frost and winds with chill factors of − 1°C (30°F) and more – especially useful for the less hardy evergreens, such as pittosporum. Knock off snow if branches seem overloaded where it is possible to reach it, but if severe cold is forecast, leave it – better one or two broken branches than a whole tree dead.

Where trees have rodent guards round the trunks during winter, these need to be inspected regularly, cold periods being when rabbits and hares will be most hungry. The height to which they can reach to gnaw bark is difficult to believe, and so is the way they will exploit gaps in the guards. Mice and voles will even have a go at bark round the trunk base if they have made nests in mulch so close to the tree that it touches the trunk.

AFTERCARE IN SPRING/SUMMER

Spring- and summer-planted trees should be carefully watched to ensure that they do not run short of water. A good watering-in after planting, and then good waterings every day, while hot dry weather continues, are essential. Conifers further need spraying with clear water so that the top growth is thoroughly wetted, each evening. Sometimes summer gales can cause wind-rock with its associated problems as in winter-planted trees.

MULCHING

During a tree's lifetime, you will get better, healthier and more orna-mental specimens if you feed and mulch them annually. Many are not so treated, certainly not if growing in the wild, and grow quite well, but ensuring that they are not short of a particular plant food, and keeping the soil in good condition, are necessary in intensively cultivated areas like gardens.

Mulching is absolutely essential. A tree produces its own potential mulch, with the annual leaf-fall, but this may be blown away, or it may be necessary to clear it off where the tree is growing in a lawn. Mulches can consist of a variety of materials besides types of bulky organic matter – black plastic sheet, sand, pebbles, even stones, anything which covers the ground – but for maintaining the structure of the soil, the bulky organics are best.

These have already been referred to in Chapter 8 for mixing with the soil in planting, but they can also be spread over the soil surface 5 or 7.5 cm (2 or 3 in) thick in a circle round the tree, to a distance of 60–150 cm (2–5 ft) from it. Put on in mid to late spring, such a mulch will have been almost completely absorbed into the soil by autumn, when the tree's own leaves can be collected and used to replace it. Leave a space round the base of the trunk so that the mulch does not touch it, otherwise it becomes a nest for small rodents.

If the tree is growing in grass, you may reluctantly have to do without a mulch, but it can be difficult to get grass to grow well in shade, and it could be that, immediately around the trunk, the soil is bare. A mulch will then prevent weeds – which will grow anywhere – from establishing.

By applying a mulch, you will maintain the soil structure, which enables the tree's roots to make the best use of the nutrients in the soil. You will keep the soil moist, prevent weeds growing, and keep up the food supply to a lesser or greater extent. Bark chippings are very good and last a long time but they, like peat, must have a balanced compound fertilizer added as well, because the quantity of nutrient they contain is minute.

FEEDING TREES

For a food supply through the growing season, an organic kind is the most useful; it breaks down slowly in the soil and nutrient is released equally slowly and continuously. Blood-fish-and-bonemeal is a good mixture, or one of the powdered seaweeds. Dried blood, hoof-and-horn or bonemeal are also good but supply only nitrogen and phosphorus, and trees need more mineral nutrients than that, especially potassium.

The compound, organic kinds will contain all three, together with the other dozen or so necessary, though in smaller quantities, as the tree requires them. Application rates will be detailed by the suppliers on the containers. If the trees are growing in heavy soil or soil already well filled with humus, the addition of fertilizers will not be necessary. When applying the material, spread it on the soil round the tree in a wide ring, remembering that tree roots can spread as far sideways underground as the top growth does above it. Time to apply is late winter–early spring.

WEED CONTROL

At all times, but especially while the trees are young, weeds should be prevented from infesting the soil round them. Ground elder, dandelions, creeping buttercup or coltsfoot, or even a dense growth of an annual like chickweed or cleavers, can seriously inhibit the growth of a young tree. Even when the ground was thoroughly cleared before planting, these weeds can all seed in again through wind, birds or insects. Keep the tree clear of them by handweeding for preference, while still small.

CHAPTER 10

SHAPING AND CONTROLLING TREES

On the whole, trees can be left to develop their natural habits of growth, and will form attractively shaped heads, provided they have been spaced far enough apart to allow them to grow to their full spread. Whereas shrubs are mostly pruned regularly every year, to encourage more flowering, and fruit trees and bushes are cut back to prevent vegetative growth dominating them at the expense of the fruiting spurs and shoots, trees need not be formally pruned. Their height would make this difficult anyway, and the need for heavy crops of fruit and flowers is not so great; in fact most trees flower profusely without any encouragement.

GENERAL PRUNING

At all times, whether young or mature, a shoot or branch which is growing more straight and vigorously than the others should be cut back to its point of origin. Do this in late autumn or winter if deciduous, and in early autumn if a conifer, in late spring if a broad-leaved evergreen, and try to do it before it becomes a major operation, otherwise it is a big shock to the tree. The only exception to these rules is the ornamental prunus (flowering cherries) which should always be pruned in late summer, whatever the reason for pruning.

Similarly, remove thin weak growth; thin out crowded shoots by removing the weakest and crossing ones first. At the end of winter, cut off dead branches or shoots, and prune tips (Fig. 5) to shoots which have died back to healthy tissue. Dead growth is brown, breaks off easily and sharply and often has cracked and peeling bark; the layer of tissue immediately below the bark will be brown, when it should be bright green. An easy test is to scrape a little of the top layer away until green, or brown, shows beneath. Paint any cut surfaces 1.3 m ($\frac{1}{2}$ in) wide and larger with a wound-sealing compound which will prevent fungal infection as well as speeding up healing.

Suckers sometimes appear, and some species are very prone to throwing them up from their roots or from the base of the trunk, for instance cherries and plums, especially if the roots are close to the soil surface. Remove them as soon as seen; they will multiply rapidly if left alone.

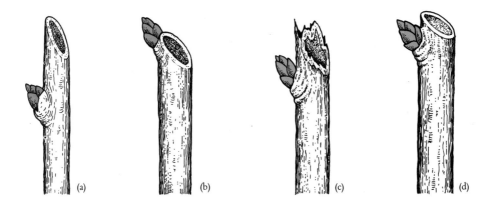

Fig. 5 Correct pruning
The three left-hand cuts are incorrect: *(a)* is too high, *(b)* is too close to the bud, and *(c)* is ragged and likely to become diseased. The correct cut, *(d)*, is just above a bud and slopes away from it to drain away rainwater.

Whether the tree is grafted on to its own rootstock or a different one, or grown as a seedling, suckers will swamp it in a few years if not dealt with, and you could easily have quite a different tree from the one you started with. Advice is generally given to pull suckers off so that the initiation point is pulled right out; if it isn't, more suckers will appear from it. But it can be difficult to do this, and sometimes impracticable, so cutting has to be done, but as close to the base of the sucker as possible.

'Water' shoots can also appear, shoots which grow from the main trunk of the tree, often low down. These, too, if left alone, can develop into a forest, absorbing the tree's strength and energy at the expense of the head. Again, prune off flush with the trunk as soon as they become obvious.

BRANCH SURGERY

If trees grow too tall, or too large all over, in spite of your care in choosing and placing them – it may be that the soil is particularly fertile or that the position is perfect – their size can be reduced. But once well grown, it is a matter of tree surgery rather than pruning, and great care is needed to ensure that the tree is not badly damaged, and that you yourself are not injured in the process. It is preferable to call in a qualified professional tree surgeon to do the job, but if it is a matter of removing a branch fairly low down, it should be possible to do this safely.

Make sure that when it comes down, it will not damage plants, fence, or wall beneath it, especially if it extends into a neighbour's garden. Make a cut with a saw through the upper side of the branch about 20 cm (8 in) out from the trunk, then another on the underside midway between it and the trunk, when it will break off. Then cut the stub back so that it is almost flush with the trunk (Fig. 6), and apply wound-sealing compound.

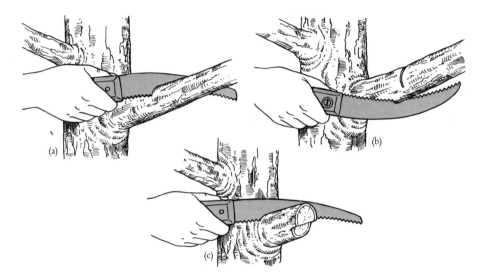

Fig. 6 Removing a branch
(*a*) Saw part way through the upper side of the branch about 20 cm (8 in) from the trunk or point of origin.
(*b*) Undercut part way through between this cut and the trunk, when the branch will snap off.
(*c*) Cut off the remaining stub almost flush with the trunk as shown.

Cutting back the roots of small trees will not be the problem that it can be with large trees, and there is no need for concern over their effects on foundations or drainpipes.

In the unlikely event that a tree has to be reduced, sadly, to a stump, strip the bark off it to kill it and either make use of it by growing a flowering climber up it – clematis, honeysuckle or roses – or reduce it to about 60 cm (2 ft), and grub it out using mattock and saw on the roots. Use the stump as a lever to rock it loose as the soil is removed.

CHAPTER 11

TREE MULTIPLICATION

Producing one's own trees is satisfying but a somewhat lengthy and complicated process. Ideally a nursery bed should be provided to bring the seedling and young trees on before they are planted in their permanent positions. For speed, it is better to buy the trees readymade, from nursery or garden centre, as it can take several years before they reach planting size. A practical problem is that cultivars, hybrids and wild varieties need to be increased vegetatively. This is often done by grafting or budding, both advanced techniques needing experience and a good deal of manual skill. They cannot be increased from seed because they will not come true to the parent, as they would if taken from a species.

However, it is much less costly to propagate one's own stock. There are further advantages in that you deal with the young tree from the start, so that you can give it the optimum conditions in which to grow while still infantile; you will know for certain that it does not have any pests or diseases and it will have come from a tree that is already acclimatized to conditions in your garden.

The simplest methods of multiplying trees: seed growing, cuttings and layering are given in the following paragraphs. Grafting has not been included for the reasons given earlier.

TREES FROM SEED

Seeds often germinate easily, and the seedlings grow comparatively quickly. It is one of the more convenient ways of propagating, but if the trees are double-flowered they will not produce seeds, or very rarely, since the reproductive parts have been converted to petals. As with all plants, seeds are at their most viable if sown when freshly ripe. Often seedlings will appear of their own accord beneath the parent trees, for instance laburnum, holly, silver birch and ash.

Hardy species can be sown outdoors in a seedbed in autumn or spring, the soil prepared first so that the top 5 cm (2 in) or so have a fine crumb structure. Space the seeds about 7.5 m (3 in) apart and sow them at a depth equal to their width. Protect them from birds with netting.

Tender species should be sown outdoors towards the end of mid spring or in late spring, or indoors in early spring. If sown under cover, use 7.5–10 cm (3–4 in) pots of potting compost, cover with black plastic sheet and keep at a temperature of about 15°C (60°F) until they germinate. Then remove the covering, but keep the seedlings at or above the same temperature during the day – it can be a little lower at night – until planting out in a nursery bed in late spring or early summer. The seeds of some tree species need special treatment called stratification before they will germinate. Put them in layers in sand or sandy compost in a pot or other container and leave them outdoors exposed to cold for the winter (Fig. 7). Trees whose seeds need stratifying before sowing include amelanchier, cotoneaster, crataegus, ilex, malus, prunus and sorbus.

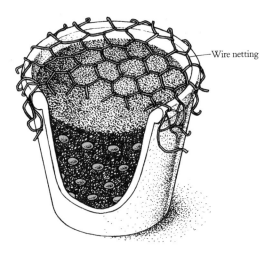

Wire netting

Fig. 7 Many tree seeds, such as holly and hawthorn, need to experience a period of severe cold before they will germinate. Arrange them in layers in a pot of sharp sand – a technique known as stratification – and stand them outdoors for the winter. Protect them from the attention of hungry mice and birds with wire netting.

While the seedling trees are in the nursery bed, keep them completely free of weeds; the competition can be great and annual weeds can even swamp a young tree completely. When moving them to their permanent positions, the thick tap or anchoring roots may break in the process, but provided there are plenty of fibrous feeding roots left, re-establishment will be good.

HARDWOOD CUTTINGS

Hardwood cuttings can also be used for propagation; these are made from young shoots produced in the same season. Cut off a 30 cm (1 ft) length from the end of the shoot in mid autumn, when the bark is brown rather than green, making the cut straight and just below a bud (Fig. 8).

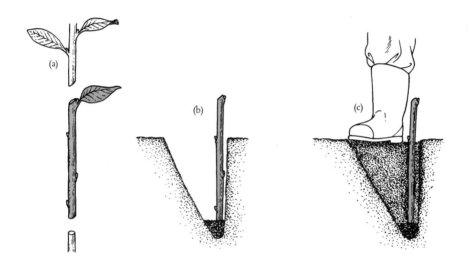

Fig. 8 Many trees can be propagated from hardwood stem cuttings inserted outdoors in late autumn.
(a) Prepare ripe woody cuttings about 23 cm (9 in) long, removing 5 cm (2 in) of soft tip just above a bud or leaf with a slanting cut. Cut straight across at the base just under a bud.
(b) Dig a narrow slit trench with one side vertical, the other sloping and spread 2.5 cm (1 in) of sharp sand in the bottom. Line out the cuttings so that two-thirds of their length will be buried and one-third exposed.
(c) Fill the trench with soil and firm in place.

Remove the extreme tip of the shoot just above a bud, then insert the cutting in a sheltered border outdoors. Make a hole about 15–17 cm (6–7 in) deep with one side slanting, put a little sand at the bottom for good drainage, and put the cutting in to half its length, then fill in firmly with crumbled soil. For insurance use a hormone rooting compound and take several cuttings rather than just one. If the cutting is evergreen, take off the leaves below soil level. Trees that can be grown from hardwood cuttings are: *Cornus kousa*, cotoneaster, euonymus, morus, *Prunus cerasifera*, salix, tamarix; note that the cotoneaster will form a mat, and needs to be grafted on to a standard stock to form a weeping tree.

HEEL CUTTINGS

Conifers are grown from heel cuttings taken in late summer. These are also made from young shoots, but they are sideshoots, between 5 and

Fig. 9 Summer cuttings under glass.

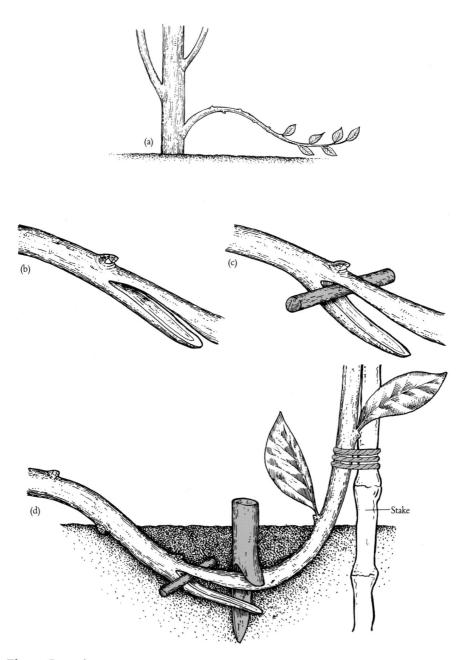

Fig. 10 Layering

(a) The shoot to be layered should be low growing.

(b) Make a slanting cut half-way through the shoot where it can be buried in the soil. The cut is made to stimulate rooting.

(c) Prop open the cut with a sliver of wood or a pebble.
(d) Peg the shoot to the ground so it cannot be disturbed by wind while rooting.
 Stake the end of the shoot upright to form a shapely new plant.

15 cm (2 and 6 in) long, and torn off rather than cut off, so that a tongue of bark is attached to the torn end. This provides a larger area from which roots can be produced (Fig. 9). The foliage is removed from the end half of the cutting, which is then put into coarse sand or a sandy compost for half its length, and kept in a closed atmosphere at atmospheric temperature until well rooted.

LAYERING

Layering is seldom used for trees, as suitable shoots are seldom produced close to the ground, but where it is, the method is to make a slanting cut partially through the underside of a current season's shoot, opposite a leaf-joint, and peg the shoot down to the soil on both sides of the cut. It is then covered with fine soil (Fig. 10), when roots will appear at the cut surface either within a few weeks or the following spring. The parent stem can be detached when the layer is well rooted, and the new plant transplanted the following autumn.

CHAPTER 12

TREE HEALTH

The best way to ensure that a tree remains in good health all its life is to give it a good start. If you can, choose a good, well-shaped strong specimen with no obvious signs of bark cracking, insect infestation, broken shoots or discoloured leaves. Plant it in a position which suits it, and where the soil and aspect are appropriate; plant it firmly and at the right time of year, and keep it supplied with water if necessary.

Provided it has been well-established, the tree's future health will then depend on possible infestation by insect pests or fungal diseases, attack by birds or mammals, and mechanical damage.

PESTS

Pests infesting trees are not as troublesome as they are on soft-tissue plants. This is just as well, since spraying even a small tree when fully grown is not easy. Provided a tree is not infested while it is young, and is healthy to start with, it will throw off a heavy infestation with the help of insect predators and parasites.

The most likely pests are various forms of aphids – greenfly, blackfly and so on – and scale insects. In warmer climates the latter may certainly be a problem; they live on the bark of the trunk and branches, and sometimes also on the undersurface of leaves and on the leaf stems.

Both insects feed by sucking the sap out of the tree, which naturally weakens it, and the secretions they produce as they feed are sticky and cover the leaves and stems. This 'honeydew' becomes a base for the growth of sooty mould , a minor fungus, and the stomata (breathing pores) of the leaves are thus blocked, again rendering the tree weak and unable to grow normally.

To some extent, birds will deal with aphids. If their numbers become acute, spraying as thoroughly as possible with permethrin will control them – this insecticide is related to pyrethrum, but is even safer as well as being more effective. Scale insects need something stronger if they get out of hand. Malathion or dimethoate, which is a leaf systemic, can be applied in late spring–early summer, or tar-oil wash in winter, when trees are completely dormant, and then only to deciduous species. This winter spray will kill adults and eggs, the late spring one only 'adolescent' scales.

Various brands of small caterpillars feed on tree leaves without much harm, and mostly get picked off by birds, but there are some much larger ones several inches long which unbelievably bore into the wood of trees and feed on it. Goat moth caterpillars feed in the trunks of mature trees, leopard moth larvae in the branches of young trees, and both do so for three or four years.

It is quite possible for a tree to be killed, but such outbreaks are fortunately rarely seen. Suspect trouble if leaves and shoots wilt on branches for no obvious reason, and look for 1.3 m ($\frac{1}{2}$ in) wide holes. Sometimes a single branch can be sawn off and destroyed, otherwise inject HCH solution into the holes, and seal them.

FUNGUS DISEASES

The notorious fungus *Armillaria mellea* has attractive honey-coloured caps to its toadstools, giving it the common name of honey fungus, but if you see these toadstools at the base of a tree trunk, it is already too late to save it – the roots will be badly infected. Honey fungus is a universal disease of woody plants, found throughout the world, living in the soil and invading trees – and shrubs – through their roots.

Slow growth, poor colour of leaves, withering of shoots during the growing season, or lack of leaves on a shoot or branch in spring, are indications that the disease may have infected. Others are black strands round the roots just below soil level, and bark which lifts easily, also at soil level, to reveal a white covering to the wood, smelling of mushrooms. The toadstools develop between mid summer and late autumn, mainly in summer.

Infected trees are difficult to treat, but it is worth trying a soil drench of a phenolic emulsion applied as the makers instruct. Otherwise a dying tree should be removed completely, particularly the roots and the black strands of the fungus, as these ensure its spread, and destroyed. If the soil in the area can be removed so much the better, but certainly no replanting should be done for at least two years.

Internal wood rots infect through pruning wounds, breakages or other injuries and the first outward symptom is wilting leaves, followed quickly by the appearance of bracket fungi from the trunk or branches, the spore-bearing part which projects in thick plate-like growths. Again control is difficult, and impracticable once the bracket stage is reached.

Coral spot exactly describes the appearance of a fungus found on dead growth, and recently more frequently on living shoots. Rounded red pimples appear on the bark, and the shoot dies back from the tip; it can easily infect through pruning wounds. Treat by cutting back as soon as seen, and destroy the prunings.

BACTERIAL INFECTION

Fireblight is a serious bacterial disease of the *Rosaceae* (prunus, malus, crataegus, etc.) which spreads rapidly in wet springs. Young leaves and tips of new shoots turn dark brown-black and look as though they have been burnt, and trees can be killed in a season. Spread is by bees and other insects, and in Britain the disease is notifiable – that is, if you suspect that a hawthorn or apple is infected, you must, in law, inform the Ministry of Agriculture, when appropriate steps will be taken to deal with it.

ANIMAL AND MECHANICAL DAMAGE

Bark gnawing by mammals occurs in winter, when the ground is frozen and they need food; hares, rabbits, mice, voles and deer are all culprits. Tree guards of wire-netting or plastic will help; deterrent sprays can also be used, especially helpful where deer are concerned and if birds are pecking off flower buds. They are harmless but unpleasant-tasting to the animal concerned.

Mechanical damage is mostly caused by extreme weather, such as wind, heavy snow or lightning. Wounds should be pared off smooth and treated with a sealing compound; bark split by frost can be taped over with insulating tape.

TREES FOR PARTICULAR SITES AND SPECIAL PURPOSES

(1) EVERGREEN
(SE = semi-evergreen)
Arbutus
Camellia
Chamaecyparis
Cotoneaster (SE)
Eucryphia (*E. glutinosa*, SE)
Ilex
Juniperus
Laurus
Magnolia grandiflora
Picea
Pittosporum
Taxus

(2) WEEPING FORMS
Betula
Cotoneaster
Fraxinus
Ilex aquifolium pendula, I. a.
  'Argentea Pendula'
Laburnum anagyroides 'Pendula'
Prunus 'Cheal's Weeping Cherry'
Pyrus
Salix caprea 'Kilmarnock'
S. purpurea 'Pendula'

(3) TREES FOR BERRIES AND
  OTHER FRUITS
Arbutus
Catalpa
Cercis
Cotoneaster
Crataegus
Euonymus
Ilex
Malus
Morus
Sorbus aucuparia cvs.

(4) TREES WITH FOLIAGE IN
  COLOURS OTHER THAN
  GREEN
Acer negundo 'Variegatum' –
  white-variegated
A. palmatum 'Atropurpureum' –
  red-purple
A. pseudoplatanus
  'Brilliantissimum' –
  salmon-pink in spring
Amelanchier – bronze-red young
  leaves
Chamaecyparis lawsoniana
  'Columnaris' – blue-grey
  C. l. 'Fletcheri' – grey-green
  C. l. 'Lanei' – yellow
  C. l. 'Pembury Blue' –
  blue-grey and green
Ilex aquifolium 'Argentea
  Marginata' – white leaf margins
  I. a. 'Mme Briot' – yellow leaf
  margins and centre
  I. a. 'Argentea Pendula' –
  white-margined weeping form
  I. a. 'Silver Queen' –
  white-margined and mottled

I. a. 'Ferox Argentea' –
white-edged hedgehog holly
I. a. 'Ferox Aurea' –
yellow-edged hedgehog holly
I. a. 'Golden Queen' – broad
yellow margins
I. × *altaclarensis* 'Golden King'
– yellow-edged leaves
I. a. 'Golden van Thol' –
yellow-edged self-fertile form
Juniperus chinensis 'Aurea' – yellow
J. communis 'Hibernica' – silvery
grey
J. communis suecica –
blue-green
J. scopulorum – blue-green
J. 'Skyrocket' – blue-green
Malus 'Profusion' – young leaves
purple
M. × *purpurea* – leaves purplish
red to purple green
Picea pungens 'Hoopsii' – silvery
blue
P. pungens 'Koster' – intensely
blue-grey
Pittosporum tenuifolium 'Garnettii' –
white-edged leaves
Prunus cerasifera 'Nigra' –
black-purple leaves
P. 'Kanzan', 'Pandora' and
'Ukon' – bronze young leaves
Pyrus salicifolia 'Pendula' – silvery
grey
Robinia pseudoacacia 'Frisia' –
yellow leaves
Sorbus aria 'Chrysophylla' – pale
yellow
S. a. 'Lutescens' – silvery-grey
when young
Taxus baccata 'Fastigiata Aurea'

(5) AUTUMN COLOUR
Acer 'Osakazuki'
Betula
Cornus
Cotoneaster
Crataegus
Eucryphia glutinosa
Euonymus
Koelreuteria
Malus
Prunus
Sorbus aucuparia

(6) FLOWERING TREES
Amelanchier
Arbutus
Camellia
Cercis
Cornus
Cotoneaster
Crataegus
Eucryphia
Koelreuteria
Laburnum
Magnolia
Malus
Pittosporum
Prunus
Salix (catkins)
Sorbus aucuparia
Tamarix

(7) PATIO TREES
Acer 'Brilliantissimum'
Amelanchier
Camellia
Cotoneaster
Juniperus 'Skyrocket'
Laurus
Pittosporum
Salix

Taxus baccata 'Fastigiata' and its
    yellow form
Prunus 'Cheal's Weeping Cherry'

(8) TREES FOR HEAVY SOIL
Acer negundo 'Variegatum'
Catalpa
Cotoneaster
Crataegus
Euonymus
Fraxinus
Malus
Morus
Pyrus
Salix
Sorbus

(9) TREES FOR POLLUTED ATMOSPHERES
Amelanchier
Betula
Catalpa
Crataegus
Fraxinus
Laburnum
Magnolia kobus
Malus
Prunus
Pyrus
Robinia
Salix
Sorbus

(10) TREES NEEDING SHELTER FROM WIND
Acer palmatum cvs.
   A. pseudoplatanus
    'Brilliantissimum'
Amelanchier
Camellia
Catalpa

Cercis
Eucryphia
Koelreuteria
Laurus
Magnolia
Pittosporum
Robinia

(11) HARDY TREES
Acer negundo 'Variegatum'
   A. pseudoplatanus
    'Brilliantissimum'
Amelanchier
Betula
Cornus

Chamaecyparis	Malus
Cotoneaster	Morus
Crataegus	Picea
Euonymus	Prunus
Fraxinus	Pyrus
Ilex	Robinia
Juniperus	Salix
Koelreuteria	Sorbus
Laburnum	Tamarix
Magnolia	Taxus

(12) TREES FOR COASTAL GARDENS
Acer pseudoplatanus
   'Brilliantissimum'
Arbutus
Betula
Cotoneaster
Crataegus
Fraxinus
Ilex
Juniperus
Pittosporum
Salix
Sorbus aria cvs.
Tamarix

INDEX